FRIENDSHIP UNLIMITED

How You Can Help a Disabled Friend

Also by Joni Eareckson Tada

Friendship UNLIMITED

How You Can Help a Disabled Friend

Joni Eareckson Tada
with Bev Singleton

HODDER AND STOUGHTON
LONDON SYDNEY AUCKLAND TORONTO

All Scripture quotations are taken from The New International Version unless otherwise indicated.

British Library Cataloguing in Publication Data

Tada, Joni Eareckson
   Friendship unlimited : how you can help a
   disabled friend.——(Hodder Christian
   paperbacks).
   1. Handicapped——Care——Religious aspects
   ——Christianity
   I. Title   II. Singleton, Bev
   261.8'324   BT732

   ISBN 0 340 42504 0

Contents

Foreword

The warm summer sun bathed the courtyard of Hilden-borough Hall. As the coach arrived, I stepped out to welcome each member of the choir who were to give a concert that evening. I went from one to another shaking hands as the whole crowd laughed and joked about not finding our centre because it was buried so deep in the jungles of Kent.

Someone behind me tapped me on the shoulder and said, "Max, meet Andrew, he's one of our best tenors." I turned to meet him with my smile ready and my hand out-stretched. As I turned and saw him my smile and hand both dropped. He was in a wheelchair. He had a warm smile but where his hands should have been, there were only twisted and deformed stumps.

There was a moment or two of awkward silence. Something deep inside me said "Help, what do I say to him? He can't possibly be a good tenor".

Another part of me, the voice of Jesus, whispered "Man looks at the outward appearance but the Lord looks at the heart. He's a person just like you. God sees no difference, and there certainly will be no difference when you get to Heaven."

I stammered out a brief "How do you do, it's nice to meet you," and felt acutely embarrassed that I could not shake his hand. Recovering my composure, I suggested that the choir unload their gear while I attend to something. I beat a hasty retreat through the front door, my thoughts busily engaged on the "something I had to attend to" – how on earth to get Andrew's wheelchair up and down the endless staircases of Hildenborough Hall. How would I get him up on stage for the concert, how would he go to the loo. I even wondered what kind of food he would eat.

My attitude to disabled people (whether they are suffering from physical, emotional or other kinds of handicap) is considerably different now. There are two main reasons for this. One is that within a few months of meeting Andrew, I found myself paralysed as the result of a car accident, and facing life in a wheelchair. The second reason is probably something much more positively formative in my experience – I read Joni's first book. Subsequently I met her and she became a good friend of our family.

Reading Joni's books and getting to know her has totally transformed many of my attitudes. I hungrily devour everything she writes. I know you will enjoy reading her new book *Friendship Unlimited* because it is so practical and so scriptural.

But more than this, the book comes from the pen of a godly woman whose life project is following Jesus. That's why the book is so powerful – it is full of exactly the kind of down-to-earth insights Jesus himself would give. This is what makes it not just another 'interesting' book but a powerful life changing dynamic, full of the gentle strength and fragrance of Christ.

I know that you will be blessed as you read it and changed as you live it out.

Max Sinclair
Hildenborough Ministries
Sevenoaks
Kent

1
We're Just People...

"How can Joni best be helped?" my parents asked the doctor after I got settled into my new room in the rehabilitation ward.

I listened as the man in the white coat and my mother and father stood at the base of my bed and talked. The doctor flipped through a chart and began the speech he'd given time and time before . . .

I was suddenly assaulted by a barrage of new words, foreign and frightful. I was a severely-involved quadriplegic with a transversal spinal lesion sustained at the fractured fourth/fifth cervical level. I would be fitted with an in-dwelling foley catheter and be given seven pills daily. I would have two hours of physical therapy a day. I was to spend time in occupational therapy. Once a week I was to go to the office of my vocational rehabilitation counselor, and twice a week to a peer group counseling session. Every kind of specialist was assigned to me—a urologist, psychologist, internist, a pulmonary specialist, and every other "ist" imaginable.

Whew!

After the doctor left, I asked someone to pull the sheet over my head and turn on the television to crowd out my frightful feelings. I peeked out from under the sheet at my roommates. One girl in a wheelchair puffed on a cigarette and stared aimlessly out the window of our ward. Another girl cracked gum, filed her nails, and waited by her food tray. Another girl, paralyzed and blind, lay in bed, her unfocused gaze fixed on the ceiling.

"Hi," I said to the girl filing her nails. "How long have you been here?"

She squinted at the ceiling, thinking. "Oh, I guess going on two years," she said matter-of-factly.

Two years! I turned my head the other way and fought back tears. This was my first day of rehab and I was already lonely. It was a world that I was neither comfortable nor acquainted with. And this was only the beginning.

Insecure and intimidated, I managed to learn the "buzz words" that seemed to be second nature to the guys in wheelchairs who hung around the elevator. Yet every time I was wheeled past them on my way to physical therapy I could barely look them in the eyes and muster a smile.

I felt the same way whenever I passed by one of the older women strapped in her wheelchair, parked by the wall. *Will that be me someday?*

I bit my lip, resolved and rigid. No. I could not . . . would not . . . believe that a successful rehabilitation would depend solely on the rehab center, its routines, and health care professionals. These people—doctors, nurses, and therapists—would surely play a profound role in helping me toward independence and acceptance.

But there had to be more.

So . . . Who Helped the Most?

What was the one thing I needed the most? Friends!

A few of those friends were merely *acquaintances*—nurses from other wards who would occasionally stop by to check in and say "hi." Other friends were *casual*—students who stopped by for an occasional visit in between classes at a nearby college. Some friends became *close*—people who visited regularly, shared common interests and visions, and helped me see beyond the hospital walls into a world that was waiting outside. Still others grew to be *intimate* friends—people who went with me to therapy, or became my advocate with the nursing supervisor, always going the second mile, giving their shirt when I asked for their coat.

Friendship Unlimited

Friendship unlimited—I could now easily answer the question my parents posed to that doctor the first afternoon at rehab. Friends—acquaintances, casual, close, or especially intimate—made all the difference in the world.

If I were to pinpoint the one common denominator these friends shared, it would be love. Love strong enough to overcome the stale, stuffy smell in my hospital room. Love strong enough to break through the fear of "having nothing to talk about." Love that refused to be squeamish when they had to empty my leg bag. And love which saw potential in me, even though I was reduced to doing not much more than writing with a pen between my teeth.

Let me share with you an example. Some time later a friend—an older man who was an extremely skilled artist—came often to challenge and inspire me through those early days of learning how to not only write, but paint while holding a brush between my teeth. He would bring in old books from his library, new kinds of paint, or different and unusual brushes.

At first I thought surely he had better things to do. Wasn't there someone more important he should be spending his time with? But he kept coming to see me.

His talent began to catch my interest. Some of the brushes he showed me were more than 30 years old—and they looked every day of it. The paint on the handles was chipped and discolored. The bristles were stubbly and uneven. If I hadn't known better, I would have said his brushes were useless—not fit for painting anything of real value.

One afternoon while giving my jaw a rest from clenching my brush, I watched him work in front of his easel.

Miraculously, in his hands the brushes became not only useful, but priceless. He swirled and swept the paint on his canvas. Each of those ugly brushes had its own purpose—one brush was for broad, thick strokes, another was for thin, straight lines.

Sitting there mesmerized, I noticed that he avoided using the new, soft sable brushes from the occupational therapy department. This artist friend of mine preferred to work with his well-worn, well-proven tools. And my friend knew his tools well—he knew what each brush could and could not do in his hands.

As a beautiful painting began to take shape on his canvas, a saying I had often heard before came to mind: *A tool unto itself is of little importance, but placed in the proper hands it can create a masterpiece.*

My gaze dropped to my paralyzed legs. It struck me that God wanted to do a similar work in my life.

Behind those institutional walls for too many months, I had begun to feel of little use and almost no value. Like a worn-out ugly thing of inferior quality and little worth. Even though that same institution did its best to help me, the rules and mechanical, day-to-day routines had barely made a crack in my tough exterior of calloused depression.

Oh sure, it was good to see some progress at physical therapy—being able to sit up in a wheelchair for five hours was a major achievement. And yes, it was helpful to make those first, shaky attempts at feeding myself in occupational therapy. The peer counseling sessions, closely monitored by a watchful professional, benefitted me some. And even my vocational rehabilitation counselor helped me open my eyes slightly to future possibilities of college and employment.

But that dear elderly man did for me what all the routines of rehabilitation could not. He gave me love— warm and personal, compassionate and accepting. Under his kind instruction I began to practice with perseverance, believing that I could actually paint as well as he said I could!

Becoming a Masterpiece

Looking back, I wish I could put myself in the shoes of that elderly man. Perhaps at first he thought that I was not fit for anything great in the kingdom of God—after all, I could do little more than clumsily slop paint on a plaster of Paris candy dish. He may have thought I was for the most part useless, having no real value to accomplish anything wonderful for the Lord. Maybe he could have assumed I had gone through too much—a rebellious period, an angry, teenaged stubborness—to look past the depressing present to the hopeful future.

But I believe my artist friend knew a precious secret, a secret that will be passed on to you in this little book. It is this: Weak and seemingly inferior people may seem to lack importance, but placed in the hands of the Master they can be a masterpiece.

The apostle Paul nearly said the same when he wrote in 2 Corinthians 4:7–12, "This priceless treasure we hold, so to speak, in a common earthenware jar—to show that the splendid power of it belongs to God and not to us. We are handicapped on all sides, but we are never frustrated; we are puzzled, but never in despair . . . Every day we experience something of the death of Jesus, so that we may also know the power of the life of Jesus in these bodies of ours" (PHILLIPS, © 1958).

Through the love and acceptance that my artist friend showed me, I, too, experienced the power of God. He walked into my room as a mere acquaintance. But over the months we became close. And now I would count him as a dear and intimate friend. The Lord used him in my life to help me understand that "though we are handicapped on all sides," we need not live in despair.

You may not be an artist with paints and brushes, but you are, no doubt, holding this book in your hands for a very special reason: you know someone disabled like me and you want to help him.

But just who are the disabled and what are we like?

We the Disabled Are . . .

Well, we make up a sizable minority. We are 35 million strong in the States. We are individuals with impairments of every shape and size . . . physical paralysis, amputated limbs, damage from strokes, pulmonary problems, hearing impairments, mental handicaps, learning disabilities, visual disabilities, and so on.

But you aren't concerned about numbers. Right now you are concerned about one special person. He is not a statistic in an attendant care manual. She is not a number on a nurse's temperature/ pulse/respiration chart. The person you have in mind is a real individual full of potential, yet often emptied of hope and a meaningful future.

The disabled person you want to reach out to may be a successful role model in his community. He may be a Vietnam veteran who's made it despite the odds, holds down a rewarding job, and leads his family.

The person you have in mind may be a business executive who recently suffered a debilitating heart attack.

He may be a boy who broke his neck at the beach—last year's high school diving champion who now manages with his zippy new sports wheelchair.

Your niece may have recently given birth to a boy with cerebral palsy. Your neighbor may have a child with cystic fibrosis. Your supervisor at work may have a son with muscular dystrophy. The boy who cleans the tables at McDonalds may be slightly mentally handicapped.

So What Can You Do?

Where can you begin to help? May I tell you where my friends began? For them, it wasn't easy . . .

I was what I would call a real *snot* when confined in the hospital many years ago. I justified my complaining and worry. After all, I was facing a life of total paralysis. I took my rotten attitude out on my friends. In fact, I was sometimes worse with those friends who were the most faithful in visiting and caring about me.

My friends would sit by my bedside, and I would lie

there in stubborn silence. They would bring a magazine, and I would shrug my shoulders and say I wasn't interested. They would offer to wheel me outside, but I would say no, I'd rather watch television. I have to admit I tested their friendship more than I care to remember!

At the same time I was trying to play games with God. I shook an imaginary fist at God and tackled Him with my questions, twisting His arm for the reasons why.

But you know what? God wasn't about to cry "uncle." In fact, my questions were child's play to Him. In His infinite wisdom, God let me go on twisting His arm until I thought I would wring it out of His shoulder. But God showed me He would not be controlled by my tactics.

Oddly, it meant a great deal that God did not condemn me for raising up questions before Him. I was under stress and in pain—and God was not insulted by my angry outbursts.

Finally I let go.

And friends were there to catch me.

At that point, friends who had a grasp of God's Word and the touch of Christ's compassion helped the most. These were the ones who didn't give up on me. With God-likeness, they refused to be held hostage by my wheelchair. They would not be controlled by my tactics. They refused to accept the guilt I pushed on them simply because of their "able-bodiedness."

Instead, they responded with an attitude that had been

shaped and molded from spending time in God's Word.

A Firm Handle on God's Word

It helped that my friends didn't whip out their Bibles from behind their backs and flip to their favorite verses. To be sure they were ready with a "reason for the hope that you have," as it says in 1 Peter 3:15. But there was no preaching. No quoting grocery lists of Bible verses. No trivializing my circumstances with trite phrases and pre-packaged advice.

First, my friends knew that God was not caught off-guard by what had happened to me. My accident was not a monkey wrench that the devil had thrown into God's plans for my life. Far from being knocked off-guard, God was not even frustrated by the devil's schemes to shipwreck my faith through my accident.

But neither were God and the devil partners in crime. Satan seeks to harm. God seeks our good and His glory. Although my paralysis seemed to raise theological questions that could not be answered, my friends could rest in God's sovereignty. They knew that although the devil powers the ship of evil, God steers that ship in such a way that all things work together for good.

It was this conviction which gave them quiet confidence in the face of my questions.

Making Hard Things from Scripture
Easy to Understand

When I began asking my friends "why," not so much with

an angry fist but out of a searching heart, I was pleased with the way they answered. No one seemed overly anxious to impress me (or themselves) with a lot of theological details. They responded as though they wanted to have a genuine conversation.

For instance, when I whined that I couldn't see how God was working things together for my good, Steve Estes, a friend of mine, answered with insight and humor.

"I bet you feel like God is running behind you with a dustpan and brush," he smiled.

I had to smile too. He described exactly how I felt.

"Better yet . . . or worse yet," he continued, "I bet you picture Him with a hammer, nails, and Elmer's glue, ready to do a patch-up job on you."

That time I laughed out loud—I was glad someone could identify. My friend was putting words to my feelings. It made me feel good that he understood. "Yeah, it's like God has come on the scene after the fact . . . like He's behind me—"

"And you've always heard that He should be leading you," Steve finished my thought.

Again, I was surprised that this guy had such empathy. And because of that empathy, I listened further.

"If that's the way you feel, welcome to the human race. Sometimes I think that God is trailing behind *me* with a broom, only able to make things right after I have been surprised by some awful problem. But the Word says differently," Steve said as he picked up his Bible. "Interested?"

I shrugged my shoulders. "Sure," I said, glad that he at least asked if I wanted to pursue it.

He opened his Bible and ran his finger down the lines of Psalm 25. "This entire Psalm is all about the Lord being out in front guiding, leading, and showing the way. And even in Psalm 23, God reminds us that He—"

"He leads me beside still waters." That time I finished his sentence.

"That's right," Steve pulled his chair closer. "God's not surprised by this—" he gestured at my bed. "You can be sure that since He's out in front of you, He's planning and preparing every step of the way."

Steve was one friend who had a firm grasp on the "reason for the hope" within him. Because he loved God and His Word, loving me was second nature. And because he was convinced of the rich storehouse of treasures in the Bible, he used his imagination to communicate that richness in creative and sensitive ways.

Do you know why I became so curious about God's Word? It was simply because I tasted something of the excitement I saw in Steve's desire for God and His Word. I wanted to know more.

You Can Begin Helping Your Friend By . . .

. . . being convinced yourself of what the Bible says about your friend's disability. Frankly, I can't think of a verse that better underscores God's sovereignty over the accidents and injuries in our lives than Romans 8:28. "And we know that in all things God works for the good of those who love him." Notice that it doesn't say all things are good. There is nothing inherently "good" about paralysis, mental retardation, or blindness. But because God is sovereign, He is able to work even sad things together for good.

How God does this is a real mystery. And when I use the word "mystery," believe it! Just consider Exodus 4:11. Moses complains to God about his own speech impairment. God replies, "Who gave man his mouth? Who makes him deaf or dumb? Who gives him sight or makes him blind? Is it not I, the Lord? Now go; I will help you speak and will teach you what to say."

And if that's not enough, take a look at Lamentations 3:32,38: "Though he brings grief, he will show compassion, so great is his unfailing love . . . Is it not from the mouth of the Most High that both calamities and good things come?"

What a mystery. But it's not a mystery without direction. There are answers. God does work things together for good. The long hours I spent in the Bible from that time onward revealed at least some of the reasons "why" behind my paralysis.

Sometime later on, Steve read a verse out of 1 Thessalonians 5:18: "In everything give thanks: for this is the will of God in Christ Jesus concerning you" (KJV).

I challenged him. "Now, wait a minute! I don't feel thankful."

"Look, Jon," he responded, "they're not saying here, 'in everything you've got to feel like a million bucks.' They're simply saying, 'in everything *give thanks*.' Lay aside those fickle feelings, push aside the emotions, dry the tears, grit your teeth if you have to, and simply give thanks."

That was a level I could hold onto. No earthly reason, no human logic, but just simple faith based on God's Word. For once in my life I looked to Jesus, the author and finisher of my faith, who for the joy that was set before Him endured His cross. Was I expected to do anything less?

That was the beginning of a long journey into the mysteries of God's will. A glimpse into His heavenly kingdom, a taste of those heavenly glories.

Is the Mystery Solved?

I still don't know all the answers.

And God doesn't expect you to have all the answers. My friend Steve couldn't respond to the toughest of my "searching heart" questions. I'm not sure I would have been satisfied to find answers to all of my questions anyway. It would have been like pouring millon-gallon truths into my one-ounce pea brain.

My friend wisely kept my focus on the Lord Jesus Christ. In so doing, I slowly came to realize that God owed me no explanations—He did enough explaining at Calvary. Romans 11 came to sum up my struggle to find answers. "Oh, the depth of the riches of the wisdom and knowledge of God! How unsearchable his judgments, and his paths beyond tracing out! Who has known the mind of the Lord? Or who has been his counselor? Who has ever given to God, that God should repay him? For from him and through him and to him are all things. To him be the glory forever!"

Your Friend Is Different

Each person, able-bodied or disabled, comes to grips with his problems differently. Don't expect the person you want to help to respond like me . . . or anyone else for that matter. Frankly, I was tired of people comparing me to Jill Kinmont, the world class skier who broke her neck and wrote a book called *The Other Side of the Mountain*. I despised the pressure of everybody's expectations. I did not want to be a role model of inspiration.

Don't be surprised if your friend refuses to fit into your expectations of what "handicapped people" are like. Disabled people are just that—people, with vices and virtues. Deal with their deepest spiritual needs as you would with anyone.

Not every disabled person is asking "why me?" Not every disabled person even wants to talk about his handicapping condition. Some have adjusted well to their impairment; others would deny that they struggle. Some disabled people see themselves as part of the "handicapped community." Others do not. Be sensitive to them as "normal" people with very "normal" needs.

A disability doesn't create new questions; it only magnifies the same ones that have been asked for ages.

We're Just People

I must close this chapter with a story about my own view of people with disabilities. It may, in fact, surprise you . . .

I was at a church recently where members of a deaf choir stood in front to sign while the hearing choir sang. The four men and five women were amazing to watch, their bodies swaying while their hands circled and swept the air, picturing each word. Each was beaming with joy—you could tell they believed the words to the hymns they were picturing although they could not hear the music.

I tried to be cool and not cry. But I could not stop the flow of tears. I was deeply moved.

Later, a young man with cerebral palsy shared his testimony. Because his speech was guttural, I had to listen intently to catch what he was saying. He mentioned lots of Scripture, and I was impressed with his handling of God's Word. Again, I cried.

That night on my way home I wondered why I was so moved. Was it pity? Compassion? Did I feel sorry for these people with disabilities different than mine? In response, a verse from Isaiah 61 came to mind. God gives to those who are broken "beauty for their ashes . . . they will be called a planting of the Lord for the display of his splendor."

So why the tears? I think it was what Isaiah was talking about—beauty for ashes. I cried to see something . . . someone so beautiful. A lovely character, a right response

to affliction, a strong witness—all borne out of brokenness. Out of what was brokenness in these people's lives,
God gave something more. He made them plantings, as
the Bible says, so that He would be glorified.

Before you read further, pray that God will use you to
help your disabled friend become the planting of the Lord.
Ask for beauty out of ashes for you . . . and then for your
friend.

1. As you build a friendship with a disabled person, do
   you see your relationship as casual, close, or intimate?
   Knowing what level of friendship you have will help
   you to meet your friend's needs more appropriately.
2. Do you think that disabled people deserve pity? What
   is your view of the "good life"? Physical perfection
   and flawless accomplishments with unending possibilities of success?
3. Do you think all disabled people have "hearts of gold"?
   Do you feel that when your friend acts ungraciously,
   he should be marked off as unappreciative of what
   everyone is doing for him?
4. Do you believe it's best to leave handicapped people
   alone—that they want to be with their own kind?
5. Do you view your disabled friend as a "project" into
   whom you can invest time and attention, hoping for

results of your labor and love? Or is your goal to love with no strings attached?

2
...So Let's Be Friends

"I don't have enough!"

That was my big excuse to my occupational therapist who was trying to teach me to write with a pen between my teeth. I was supposed to practice writing the alphabet, but all I could do was complain, "I don't have enough control."

Actually I was scared to death to even try. What if I failed? If I couldn't do something as simple as writing with a pen in my mouth, then what in the world *could* I do?

Then one afternoon in the occupational therapy room, I watched another young quadriplegic with a pen held between his teeth. He had fewer functioning muscles than I and wore a special brace to support his shoulders. He could barely turn his head to look at me. But there he sat with that pen between his teeth making very hesitant, yet bold lines on a piece of paper.

I was impressed not so much with his ability as with his courage. Watching him gave me the very push I needed. And you know what? With practice, my mouth writing became as clear and concise as my handwriting. I discovered I had more than enough control. I had enough muscles. All those times I complained that I didn't have what it took were nothing but lame excuses.

Many of us complain about not having enough. We don't have enough money. We're not smart enough or talented enough.

Do you feel that way when it comes to being a friend to a disabled person? Are you fearful that you don't understand what being a real friend entails? Are you concerned you don't have enough social expertise to deal with someone else's handicap? You don't have enough skill, background, or knowledge?

So much is not accomplished—not even attempted—because we're afraid of failing. But that's only natural. We don't try because we're afraid of hurting the other person, or stumbling over the right words to say. Maybe our disabled friend will be even more aware of his handicap if we make a mistake. So we stay out of the way—completely!

Don't be afraid—you have more than enough. If you're a child of God, you have His Holy Spirit. And 2 Peter

1:3 says, "His divine power has given us everything we need for life and godliness." If you have the Lord Jesus, you have enough. Much more than you think can be achieved with what you've already been given.

Take heart. No one expects you to be a model of perfection. And no one can argue with love that is sincere and compassionate, even if you do stumble over your words.

Getting Rid of Fear

We can learn a lot from children about opening up to other people. After all, Jesus even told us to become like little children. Honest . . . open . . . questioning . . . accepting. That's the way kids are, isn't it?

For example, a funny thing happened to me at the supermarket last Saturday. I gave part of my shopping list to a store clerk who proceeded to collect my groceries. While he was busy, I wheeled toward other aisles to get a few extras that weren't on my list. Usually I look for a friendly face on a woman or child—someone who can easily reach a can of vegetables or box of detergent.

While I maneuvered down one of the crowded aisles, carefully avoiding the stacks of paper towels on display, I passed a little boy who was not more than four years old. He was sitting in front of his mother's cart, surrounded by quarts of milk and bags of fruit.

I smiled as I whizzed past him in my chair. He was a few feet behind me when I heard him call, "Hey, how did you get your motorcycle in here?" I could hear stifled chuckles up and down the aisle.

How's that for an open greeting? He couldn't quite figure out the difference between a motorcycle and a wheelchair, but he voiced an honest, friendly question. And it revealed a healthy attitude toward my disability. In fact, I got the impression that he would have enjoyed sitting in my wheelchair and putting it into high gear!

Kids know how to break the ice—they dive right in! Sometimes we adults need to do the same.

Being Disabled Doesn't Mean You're Sick

Pity is not the kind of attention any of us want. Once a man sat down next to me, patted my knee, and sighed, "Oh, it's no fun being sick, is it?"

I gave him a curious look. "Uh . . . I don't have a cold or anything."

"No, no, no." He shook his head. "It's that wheelchair. I'm sorry you're sick," he said insistently.

I felt my defenses rising, but bit my lip before I spoke. "Please sir, I want you to know that being in a wheelchair doesn't automatically make me sick," I said with gentle persuasion.

"Is that so?"

I nodded and smiled. I could tell a new attitude was taking shape.

Countless opportunities like that have given me the chance to set the record straight in people's minds. So please be mindful to treat a disabled person as a healthy individual. Just because the person has a functional limitation does not mean he is sick or diseased. Cerebral palsy is not a disease—it's any of several disorders of the nervous system. A broken neck or back is not an illness—it is an injury to the spinal cord. Polio is not a sickness—it is a handicapping condition which results from a virus. True, some disabilities are accompanied by health problems. But for the most part, disabilities are simply conditions or impairments.

What about Greeting Someone Who Is Disabled?

A good rule of thumb: Treat a disabled person in the same way you would any able-bodied person you are meeting for the first time. You may be waiting in the grocery line together . . . attending the same party . . . next to each other at a PTA meeting . . . sitting near each other in Sunday school. Discuss the sorts of things you would normally. Smile . . . ask his name . . . where she is from, and so on. Converse naturally. Don't feel you must ask about the disability—especially if you sense he is uncomfortable with his handicap, or unwilling to discuss it.

On the other hand, it may be wise not to ignore the person's disability either. In some cases, such as with those who are deaf or non-verbal, it's impossible to avoid—if you don't acknowledge the disability, how will you communicate?

If it seems natural to open up the topic of disabilities, it can be appropriate to ask sensitive questions. Most disabled people don't mind helping you to understand. You might say something like . . .

"Pardon me, may I ask you a personal question? How did you become paralyzed?"

"Excuse me, but I'm interested in your disability. Could you tell me how you came to be in a wheelchair?"

Of course, the key word is *appropriate*. There may be times and places when such questions come up in the middle of a conversation. Use common sense. Be sensitive. Never ask questions out of morbid curiosity; ask because you want to communicate care and interest.

Should I Shake Someone's Hand or Not?

One afternoon when my girlfriend and I were visiting a shopping mall, I noticed a large woman and a shorter man, arm in arm, walking toward me. As they drew nearer, the man's face brightened.

"Aren't you the lady who paints with her mouth?" he said as he extended his hand toward me.

"Why yes, I—"

"Don't do that!" the woman hoarsely whispered as she smacked his wrist. "Don't you know she can't feel?!"

"Please, I don't mind—" I began to say.

She jerked his elbow and pulled him away, shaking her finger. The man looked over his shoulder and meekly waved goodbye. I sighed and shrugged my shoulders. What could have been a pleasant exchange between the man and me was rudely aborted. If only the woman had approached our encounter with common sense. If it is natural for you to shake a person's hand, then feel free to shake the hand of a person who's in a wheelchair.

But, you may say, what if the person has a prosthetic arm such as a metal hook for a hand? Then feel free to shake his hook, especially if he extends the prosthesis toward you. Don't be concerned at grasping a piece of cold metal and giving it a pleasant shake—the disabled person considers that piece of metal his "hand." However, if you have second thoughts or feel too awkward, reach for his other hand or shoulder.

If the person is not capable of raising his paralyzed hand to you, go ahead and reach for it anyway, giving it a gentle squeeze. But I must underline the word "gentle." Some people struggle with painful arthritis in their hands.

Incidentally, people who are blind need you to take the initiative and reach out to them—often they will extend a hand and expect you to respond.

Usually I lift my arm so people can shake my hand. I can't feel their grasp. My fingers cannot naturally intertwine with theirs. Sometimes they only hold my wrist. (Children shake my two fingers!) Whatever "handshake" method you choose, it's the gesture that counts, closing the distance between two people. Touching communicates acceptance and warmth.

Eye-to-Eye Conversation

I've occasionally noticed that people's eyes start drifting downward when they are talking to me. They are mouthing words, but I can tell their attention is on my legs or my hands resting on my lap. I can almost tell what they are thinking. How does she keep her legs in shape? I wonder if her shoes show wear on the soles? Why do her fingers curl so?

All of us, able-bodied and disabled, enjoy eye-to-eye conversations. It is especially important to remember this when meeting a disabled person—more so when the muscles in his face are tightly drawn in contortion. If the person has lost control of certain facial muscles, he may have difficulty swallowing and may drool. If you look that person in the eyes, you soon forget their deformities. Do you remember the saying, "The eyes are the window of the soul"? Looking at a person in this way, you appreciate their heart, and forget their appearance.

God does the same with us. He reminded Samuel, "The Lord does not look at the things man looks at. Man looks on the outward appearance, but the Lord looks at the heart."

The conversation widens if the disabled person has a companion with him. Don't forget the person who is standing behind the wheelchair. Often he or she remains in the shadow of his disabled friend. On the other hand, don't carry on a monologue with the companion. View these people as separate individuals. Don't always assume that they are a "pair" who enjoy the same interests or have the same opinions.

Treat a person age-appropriately, using the same tone of voice as you would if they were able-bodied. Please be careful not to "talk down" to those of us with physical disabilities. The following is virtually a transcript of an actual conversation.

"Oh, dearie, you look so *sweet* today," the lady in the large print flowered dress said as she stooped and patted my cheek.

"Yes . . . well, thank you," I stammered.

"You always look so pretty. And your nails!" she pressed her hand to her cheek.

"My nails?" I looked to see what she thought was so unusual.

"Well I must be going," she stroked my hair. "Ta."

I wonder if that woman would have conversed that way if I were standing up. Somehow I can't imagine her stroking and patting me, a 38-year-old woman, if I were on my feet. Be mindful not to treat disabled people like children. *Deal with a disabled person on an age-appropriate level.*

Offering a Helping Hand

Recently I was wheeling on an airport crosswalk, my lap and foot pedals loaded with luggage. A man ran up behind me, tucked his briefcase under his arm and grabbed my wheelchair handles.

"Here, let me give you a hand," he shouted above the traffic as he threw his weight behind my chair. Before I could respond, the front wheels abruptly stopped against the lip of the curb, throwing me and my luggage forward.

Packages were scattered everywhere. The man scrambled to gather my things. "I'm so sorry . . . I'm so sorry."

I could tell his motive to help was sincere. But I warned him against future catastrophes, saying, "It's okay. Just make sure next time you ask before you act."

As you would for anyone, please do offer your assistance if you see a way to help. If you spot someone wheeling his chair toward a door, simply ask, "Do you need some help?" Offering assistance is a common courtesy. Wait for a reply, though, before going ahead. And if the person says, "No, thanks," that's okay. At least you have offered.

Some Other Examples

You may come across someone who is blind standing by an elevator. It's okay to ask if you may press the floor button for them, especially if the buttons are not marked in Braille. It's also thoughtful to hold the elevator door open for someone less ambulatory as they make their way out onto the floor.

Paraplegics in wheelchairs are able to grocery shop independently but may need help with items from the top shelves or to reach the scales to weigh their fruits and vegetables.

You can hold a hymn book for another, help a blind person across the street, or assist a woman with a cane up the stairs. However, you should also realize that many of these disabled people would not be out in public if they weren't able to manage, for the most part, on their own. You'd be surprised how independent blind, deaf, and physically handicapped people really are when it comes to making their way in the mainstream.

Minor emergencies, though, do happen. You might be asked to pick up something that has been dropped, push a wheelchair that has lost its power, dial a phone for someone who is deaf . . . the possibilities are unlimited. Your willingness and availability is a demonstration of Christ's love to those in need.

The Inside Scoop

May I share a few more helpful hints? When you encounter someone in a wheelchair for the first time, please don't casually put your foot up on the wheel or hang on the armrest. I don't know how to explain it other than to say that a wheelchair is part of a person's body space. Hanging or leaning on a wheelchair is similar to leaning on a person sitting in a chair. That kind of familiarity is reserved for close friends who find it comfortable to hug or embrace occasionally.

And remember our necks! When people approach me who are very tall, sometimes I get a crick in my neck after speaking with them for awhile. For better visibility, stand a few feet away. That puts us more on the same level. Also, you will want to stand directly in front of a person who cannot turn his head to the side due to inflexible neck muscles.

If you are going to have a long conversation, the very best idea is to pull up a chair and sit eye level with someone in a wheelchair. It makes it a lot easier to carry on a conversation face to face.

These suggestions may seem obvious to you, but you'd be surprised how many people scratch their heads, wondering what to do in the same situations.

Getting into a Conversation . . .
with Someone Who Can't Speak!

One morning after church a young woman with cerebral palsy approached me in her wheelchair. Her speech was difficult to understand and she kept repeating a certain sentence over and over. Even though I patiently asked her to slowly repeat each word, I still could not understand. I couldn't tell if she was in terrible trouble or was simply trying to communicate an exciting experience.

Finally, I got the message. She wanted me to help her find someone who could assist her into the restroom. A simple request. And I felt so helpless, so inadequate, because I took so long to understand her. But I sure did rush to get her help!

That incident helped underscore the importance of learning to communicate with someone who cannot speak, somebody who has cerebral palsy or has suffered a stroke.

Sure, it's uncomfortable to go up and greet someone only to discover they cannot talk. Don't panic. Your friend who cannot speak has encountered nervous people like you a hundred times before. Consider it a challenge the two of you will work out together. Your friend probably would be encouraged, too, if you admitted, "You know,

I've never done this before. That is, talk to someone whose words I can't understand. But I'd sure like to try."

The first step? Ask if they have a word board. A word board is a communication device, commonly used by non-verbal people. It may have letters of the alphabet which a person can point to in order to construct a sentence. Other word boards list commonly-asked questions such as, "May I have a drink of water?" or "Would you find my attendant?" Another communication device is a small computer which prints a message as the person pushes certain keys.

If he doesn't have a word board, go to the next step. Find out what his sign or signal is for "yes" or "no." Begin by asking, "What's your signal for 'yes'?"

In response, he may look up at the ceiling . . . shake his foot . . . wink once . . . or any number of other signals. When you spot the sign, you might say something like, "Is winking once your sign for 'yes'?" And they'll wink once. Easy.

Once you both understand the common language, you can carry on a regular conversation by playing twenty questions. Find out his name, find out his interests. I have often said, "My name is Joni. I'd love to know what your name is. Does it start with an A, B, C, D . . . ?" I continued until I was able to spell the person's name. (I hoped it wasn't Zelda!)

There may be a time when a non-verbal person approaches you with a special need. Just ask some basic questions. It would assure them if you said, "I cannot understand you. I'm going to try to figure out what you're saying. First of all, are you in any kind of pain?"

They might say or sign, "no."

You can continue, "Do you need something?"

And again their response is "no."

"Is there anything wrong with your wheelchair?"

They might shake their head "yes."

"Would you like me to take the brakes off?" Take a closer look at his wheelchair. "Is your cushion uncomfortable?" Take it from there, asking basic questions.

Like my story of the girl who needed help to the restroom, it may not be easy to understand what your new friend is trying to tell you. But he will understand that you cared enough to stop, to be real with him, to be quiet, and to listen.

Labels

Wouldn't it be awful if your worst insecurities, the things you most struggled with, were written on a label and stuck to your back? Out in the open for all the world to see and poke fun at? Maybe your label would say "fat" or "too tall." Someone else's label might read "too short" or "too skinny." Worse yet, wouldn't it be awful if your label said something like "This person is paranoid" or "This person is poor."

Thankfully, labels like these are not stuck to you with glue. You can pull them off, crumple them up, and throw them in the wastecan where they belong.

But other labels aren't so easy to dispose of. They are

just as painful and humiliating. But unfortunately, these labels can't be peeled off and discarded.

A lady from out of state wrote me about her daughter who has Downs syndrome. She mentioned in her note that she and her husband have become keenly sensitive to the experiences of the disabled. Then she edited herself and suggested the word "handicapped." Then, as if holding a red pencil, she made one more change. She scribbled in a bunch of question marks as if to say she wasn't certain *what* word to use. In frustration, I pictured her throwing her hands up in the air. The woman lamented that she didn't know which word was least likely to be read as a derogatory label.

I can appreciate this mother's predicament. Nobody wants to purposefully stick a label on another. Labels tend to limit people, boxing them into categories in the minds of others. Labels foster negative impressions. They segregate . . . separate.

Even acceptable words like "disabled" or "handicapped" or "impaired" or "physically challenged" can become sticky labels when we refuse to see these people as persons first—individuals with hopes and dreams, opinions and interests. We need to view people with disabilities as persons, not conditions. "She's a deafie" or "He's a retard" are labels that communicate more harm than good. Those statements say that the handicap is more obvious than the person. Instead, it would be better to say, "The girl who is deaf" or "The boy who is mentally retarded."

There are a few more careless words that are negative

or just plain inaccurate. So that you can steer clear of such words, here are some no-no's from the dictionary of the disabled.

Avoid the word "afflicted." Many disabled people feel that word makes them out to be victims. "Cripple" and "invalid" also have negative connotations.

"Burden" or a "drain" are more words to avoid. Many disabled people don't consider their impairment a burden. The disability simply presents a few added responsibilities.

Be careful how you use the word "suffers." "She suffers from blindness" or "He suffers from a spinal cord injury" just may not be true. If a person with a disability is independent and copes with life successfully, then that word does not apply any more than it would for an able-bodied person. To tell you the truth, I suffer a lot more when I have the flu than when I cope with my everyday routines in a wheelchair.

Disabled people are not "handicaps" or "poor unfortunates." What's unfortunate is that these words are often used to describe people who live happy and meaningful lives.

A person who is handicapped is not necessarily a "victim." Let's be mindful that his disability has been permitted by God for a very special reason.

My goal in giving you this list is to ask your aid in keeping disabled people from sounding pitiful or inferior. If we can avoid using these words in everyday language, then

we'll do a great service to the disabled community. And
go a long way toward correcting our own attitudes at the
same time.

How Can You, an Able-bodied Person, Really Identify?

Comfort. What does that word bring to mind? A time when
a friend held you close, not saying a word, while you
quietly cried? Your mother's lap after you fell off your
bike? Her gentle touch when she brushed the stones away
from your knee with a wet cloth while soothing you with
her words? How about that time you sat with your neighbor
at her kitchen table? With your hands wrapped around a
steaming mug of coffee, you opened up about your
mother's illness. And she listened.

We have a way of remembering the consolation we
receive from people who care. God gives them the right
words to say. His love and grace flows through them
to us.

2 Corinthians 1:3–4 talks of that comfort. "Praise be
to the God and Father of our Lord Jesus Christ, the Father
of compassion and the God of all comfort, who comforts
us in all of our troubles, so that we can comfort those in
any trouble with the comfort we ourselves have received
from God."

Notice that verse doesn't say we can only comfort
those with whom we can identify. It says we can comfort
those in *any* trouble—any heartache, any disease or
injury. That should take away any insecurity when we

are called upon to give comfort to someone with troubles greater than our own. God says it's possible. He is our enabler.

In the years since my injury, I've come to see that a person usually isn't ready for advice just after something drastic has happened to him. Looking back on my own experience, I don't think my "why?s" were very sincere for the first year or two. It took awhile to sort through my feelings and emotions. Then, and only then, was I able to honestly search for some answers.

Your new friend may be asking those same questions I threw out at family and friends. "Why in the world did this happen to me? . . . Why?" They may not be looking for advice. Instead, they need and want comfort.

This is the time to do what the Bible says—"Weep with those who weep." It doesn't say to tell them, "Dry those tears and shape up." That's a happy-go-lucky, unrealistic approach. But the Bible is a *real* book written to *real* people. And people deserve a real response. Giving comfort is sometimes a better response than giving advice.

Don't bite your nails thinking you have nothing to say to a quadriplegic. Don't walk away thinking you can't help your neighbor with a cystic fibrosis baby because you have healthy children. Your family may have no one with a disability, but you *can* give comfort to people in *any* situation.

Giving Comfort . . . Not Advice

My husband was on the phone the other night. Even though he was in the other room, I could tell from the tone of his voice that the conversation was strained.

I heard Ken hang up. It was silent for a few minutes and then he came into the room.

I was sitting in bed, propped up with pillows with an open book balanced on my lap. I didn't mind interrupting my reading. Ken had a lot on his mind.

"Do you want to talk?" I asked.

"Yes . . . I think so."

He sat on the edge of my bed and began to unfold his feelings. A half hour of this one-sided conversation went by before Ken stood up, stretched, and commented he was feeling a lot better.

When he walked out of the room, I marveled. I helped him and I hadn't said a word the entire thirty minutes.

All I did was listen.

But I don't always listen well. That experience reminded me that there is a real difference between hearing and listening. I was reminded that it is possible that God gave us one mouth and two ears as a clue for us to listen twice as much as we talk.

There's something comforting about sharing memories. Especially if you're disabled and have fond memories of days when you weren't always in a wheelchair. Even the apostle Paul wrote from prison to his friends and reassured them that his suffering was soothed by the joy of memories. He started out his letter to the Philippians, "I thank God every time I remember you."

Nice memories . . . I still like to talk about them. They have a way of bolstering our spirits and inspiring us through long stretches of difficulties.

I thank the Lord for friends who don't mind listening if I feel like recounting memories. I remember the feel of my wet feet walking on the warm concrete apron of a swimming pool. I remember the feel of wet leather reins in my hands when I would ride my horse. And on a hot day it was a relief to feel the chill of an ice cold bottle of Coke in my grip. When I would jog with my friends, I recall the exhausting, yet exhilarating sensation of working muscles.

Snapping flowers off their stems. Scouring a sink with sponge and cleanser. Creaming my own hands. Having my ankles rubbed. My fingers on the ivory keys of a piano. Brushing a horse's coat. Drumming my fingers on a desk. These, and so many other remembrances, help me to not take for granted those things I still can feel and do. And their joy is multiplied if shared with a friend . . . a listening friend. What comfort!

Continuous Giving

But what if you give and give, and nothing happens?

The story is not all that uncommon. It may be like an experience which a woman recently shared. She was very discouraged with her neighbor who was disabled. It was distressing to spend a great deal of time and effort trying to get her neighbor friend to come to church with no response.

Perhaps, she thought, her disabled friend would rather go to the park or a local shopping mall. Still her offers were kindly refused.

The woman questioned me, "What is the matter? What am I doing wrong? How come I can't get her out of the house?"

There are no easy answers to those questions, but there may be a few insights to consider. The following account may help shed light on the problem.

As the Allied forces marched into Germany and Poland after World War II, they freed prisoners as they traveled east. As they approached the concentration camps, the Allied armies threw open the gates and tore down the barbed wire fences to release the captives. The people who had been constrained behind those prison walls for years were free . . . free to go back to their homes, back to their cities and their countries.

But a startling thing happened. Those people, some half starved and defeated in spirit, stood there at the open gates for a moment. Then they turned around and headed back to their cells, refusing to face the freedom head-on.

What does this show? People are most secure in surroundings which are familiar to them. That prison had become a home to some of those people. It was the only thing about which they had first-hand knowledge.

In the same way, I can understand that the neighbor with a disability was facing the same dilemma. She was familiar with her home . . . with the rooms, with the walls. She was comfortably acquainted with her day-to-day routines. Anything out of the ordinary like a trip to a local mall or a visit to a nearby church could be threatening to her cozy, almost sequestered, tedium.

The sameness of a room with four walls is a comfort when you're deeply acquainted with every nook and cranny. It has no surprises.

Now consider the surprises outside the room. There are very real barriers, visible and invisible, to consider before taking your friend beyond his familiar boundaries. Some of the barriers are architectural like stairs and narrow doorways. But the more painful barriers are the attitudinal ones like pity or rejection, stares or avoidance tactics.

Little wonder a disabled person fears facing life out in public. Yet fear, although a natural and an honest response, should never stop a person from getting into the mainstream of life.

There was a time I struggled with the same thing. My friends helped me push past those fears during the first few jaunts out of my home.

Joined by friends with whom I was especially at ease, we began with short outings like wheeling down to a local park or having a picnic. They would check to see if a museum or art gallery nearby was accessible to wheelchairs.

Hurdling the small obstacles prepared me for more challenging ventures. No longer did I shrivel under the stares of people around me whenever a friend would lift a hamburger to my mouth. I didn't mind when my friends pushed aside clothes racks in order to wheel me through the aisles of a dress shop. I had confidence!

Next thing I knew, my friends were standing in line with me at the registrar's desk at a local college, helping me select courses, and organizing volunteers to take notes. My friends helped me overcome the fear of eating in the college cafeteria. They made me at home at the student union. Each step drew me closer to real emotional health. And, best surprise of all—I even felt better about myself.

So my advice to the woman who wants to help her disabled neighbor to get out into public? Why not take a look at 1 John 4:18 where it talks about perfect love casting out fear. Then pray that you can show God's love in such a way as to dispel your friend's fears. Keep knocking on her door. Keep asking her out. That sort of persistence will pay off, and you both will benefit from a deeper and broader friendship . . . a friendship that goes far beyond the walls of her own home.

BLESSED are you who take the time to listen to difficult speech, for you help me to know that if I persevere I can be understood.

BLESSED are you who never bid me to "hurry up" and take my tasks from me and do them for me; for often I need time rather than help.

BLESSED are you who stand beside me as I enter new and untried ventures, for my failures will be outweighed by the times I surprise myself and you.

BLESSED are you who ask for my help, for my greatest need is to be needed.

BLESSED are you who understand that it is difficult for me to put my thoughts into words.

BLESSED are you who encourage me with a smile to try once more.

BLESSED are you who never remind me that today I asked the same question two times.

BLESSED are you who respect me and love me as I am, just as I am, and not like you wish I were.

—Anonymous

3
I Wish You'd Ask...

It happened to me, and it happens to almost every disabled person I know . . .

The scene was the airport. The gate agent transferred me onto a narrow aisle chair in order to wheel me on board the airplane. My two friends had boarded the plane ahead of time to stow their carry-on luggage under the seats and in the overhead bins. Of course, we all knew our assigned seat numbers.

As the agent wheeled me through the jetway, I mentioned our seat numbers to him. He grunted and continued wheeling me until we arrived at the door of the plane. The flight attendant asked for my seat assignment. Again I mentioned the number.

The agent did not budge. He refused to take me on board. I explained again that I knew where I was to be seated. But he insisted he wanted to double-check with my friends. As we sat there waiting, I knew why he didn't believe me.

It's happened many times. People see my paralyzed body and make the mistake of assuming that my brain is paralyzed too. They observe that I am dependent on others and thus reason I must rely on those same people to make my decisions. To do my thinking.

I wish he would have asked. Like he would have asked anyone who could stand on two feet.

That man's unwillingness to take my word hurt me deeply, and I struggled hard against the insult. Yet many of my disabled friends meet with this kind of humiliation every day. They rub shoulders with people who don't care what they have to say. Worse yet, *no one ever asks*. No one asks for an opinion, for information, for directions . . . for anything! Disabled people have so much to say—even about their handicapping conditions—but so few take the time to ask them questions.

The gate agent probably assumed I was mentally handicapped because he had no idea that spinal cord injury does not affect my thinking. He could have learned something from a handicapped manual, but who has time for that?

Now, I have no intention of writing a manual filled with medical jargon. I don't want to unload a volume of facts. Rather, I'd like to share enough info to give you a handle on the various handicapping conditions so you will have a better understanding about your friend's disability. Learning a few facts can make all the difference in shaping a healthier attitude. And you'll be better equipped to reach out in the most effective way with Christ's love.

Physical Handicaps

When it comes to asking and answering questions about handicapping conditions, nobody does it better than kids. No topic is sacred!

Take my own paralysis. Come to think of it, even the word "paralysis" raises questions of its own. For children—or adults, for that matter—the word sounds frightening, yet very mysterious. A child's first question (yet not voiced until the third or fourth!) is how I manage in the bathroom. Others will notice my leg spasms and wonder how I can move—since I can't move!

A few kids think that being paralyzed is the same as being stiff or rigid. One boy asked if my body remained in the same sitting position when I was in bed. Of course, they always scratch their heads when they learn I can drive a van 65 miles an hour on the freeways.

Spinal cord injury

I had many of the same questions when I was admitted to the rehab hospital after my diving accident. There were people of every age on my wing. All of us were there because of spinal cord injury. Some were straining to push their wheelchairs while others whizzed by in zippy power models. Still, others were in bed with paralysis too limiting to even sit up. A few shuffled down the halls with walker aids. And there were those whose paralysis was much like mine—severe, but at least I was able to sit up.

It seemes strange at first. All of us were classed as having spinal cord injury, and yet we were so different. That prompted me to ask my doctor a lot of questions. His explanation cleared my thinking and will help you, too.

He told me the spinal cord is a bundle of nerve fibers and cells which connects the brain with muscles, skin, and internal organs. An injury, permanent or temporary, results when one of the vertebrae in the spinal column breaks and either bruises or cuts the cord.

The spinal cord can be injured at any point along its approximate 25 inches. Depending on the location of the damage, each injury has its own unique characteristics. Occasionally the cord will be severed completely. Most often it will be badly bruised. Depending on which combination of "wires" remains intact, a wide range of functioning abilities results.

A total severance of the spinal cord means a person cannot feel or generate movement below the level of injury. Also, the higher the injury point, the greater loss of function. That's why some folks are up and about in walkers and others are hooked up to respirators simply in order to breathe. Functioning with a broken neck is quite different than functioning with a broken back.

For instance, a *paraplegic* is one who has sustained an injury in the lower part of the spinal column, perhaps at the chest or lower back level. And the prefix "para" means half of the body is involved.

Quadriplegia, on the other hand, involves all four limbs of the body. A lesion (injury) in the spinal cord at the upper portion of the spine will usually result in paralysis of both arms and legs.

Although a great deal of research is going on right now to find a cure for spinal cord injury,* the paralysis is usually permanent. The cord is unable to regenerate or repair itself. Unless a cure is developed (and unless the Lord intervenes with a divine healing!), people with SCI (a nifty abbreviation) can expect to deal with functional limitations.

There are nearly 250,000 persons in the United States who now are paralyzed as the result of a spinal cord injury. And every year 8,000 more are added. The number keeps going up because people in the States have a very active, mobile lifestyle. You may be called upon to help those in your circle of family and friends who have experienced a spinal cord injury.

And don't worry about asking questions. Remember though, each paralyzed person will answer differently. Some of my best friends who are quads have vastly different opinions on their disabilities and personal routines.

---

*For more information on spinal-cord injury research, contact the American Paralysis Association, 1047 Gayley Avenue, Suite 202, Los Angeles, CA 90024.

Perhaps that's why you need to ask questions.

How can you best help her? You'll never know until you ask. Say, for instance, you are dining with a SCI person for the first time. The conversation may run something like this . . .

"Hamburgers look good, don't they?" Jennifer said as she leaned on her wheelchair armrests to get a good look at the menu.

"Are you planning to order one?" Melissa asked.

"No," her friend sighed, "I'm really not that hungry."

Melissa knew that was not the case. She prayed for the right words, not wanting to force her friend to do more than she could. "Jennifer, you mentioned you were hungry just an hour or two ago. I don't want to force you, but if you're willing to order something, I'm willing to help."

"Well . . . uh," Jennifer sighed, "my hands don't work well enough to grab a big-sized burger."

"Hey," Melissa said, "No problem, I'll be happy to give a hand. Just let me know what to do."

The girl in the wheelchair smiled demurely. "That's okay," she said in a polite whisper, glancing at the other patrons in the restaurant. "I really would rather not be fed. You know, it just looks . . . well, funny. Besides, I'm not very neat," she concluded her argument.

Melissa reached over and touched the armrest of her friend's wheelchair. "I understand. But if you're really into hamburgers, I can easily cut the entire thing up for you, bun and all. You can handle it using your special spoon."

Jennifer seemed surprised at the suggestion. "You'd do that? Uh . . . thanks. I guess I *will* order a double burger with extra onions after all," she laughed. There was a thoughtful pause. "You know, I was expecting you not to understand my feelings . . . thought you'd give me a lecture about being fed in public. Thanks for being a friend, a real friend."

The girl in our story used a special spoon. You see, many disabled people are able to feed themselves. A burger may have to be cut up, a glass may have to be lifted, or a napkin may have to be unfolded and placed in a lap, but many manage very well with only occasional help.

But suppose our story went differently . . .

Camille wasn't sure how she and her disabled friend, Nadine, ended up in a restaurant. She was only planning to wheel Nadine to the mall. But here they were, and Camille nervously surveyed the table. What should she do first?

"Mind spreading my napkin on my lap?" Nadine suggested.

Of course, Camille thought to herself, *silly me—why didn't I think of that?*

"Mind if I look at the menu with you?" said Nadine.

Camille was losing what little appetite she had. All she could think of was how stupid she felt. She bravely asked the obvious question, "What do you plan to order?"

Nadine glanced over the page. "A hamburger with extras," she said smiling. "You don't mind feeding me, do you?" she said with a confidence which surprised Camille.

Camille hesitated. "Great, but . . . uh, I've never fed anybody a hamburger." She could just see herself smashing too much of the hamburger into her friend's mouth, squirting ketchup everywhere, and scattering french fries on the floor. She took another deep breath and then said, "Mind if you're a guinea pig?"

"You'll do fine," Nadine said to put her friend at ease.

"Okay, but just let me know when you want a bite."

Her friend in the wheelchair leaned forward as if to share a secret. "We can shorten it—when you see me finish a bite, then just give me another!"

A conversation like this can happen anytime. Sometimes the able-bodied helper confidently knows what to do; other times, the disabled person gives all the helpful directions. As was already shared, disabled people have different ways of dealing with different situations.

I want to re-emphasize the importance of allowing your handicapped friend to do as much as she can for herself. If she is learning to feed herself, let her. Even if she spills and drops things, encourage her anyway. As her friend, you can gently nudge her toward greater independence.

Above all, keep a sense of humor! Things will go wrong, so learn not to take these circumstances too seriously. Flat tires on the wheelchair, the insensitivity of people, leaking leg bags, inaccessible buildings, spilled food, spasms . . . even one of these can send us into a tailspin on our best of days if we let it. So learn to laugh.

For example, let me tell you about one of "those" times. I had been asked to speak at a conference and had been introduced on stage. As I was making my way to the microphone, I realized I still had a big wad of bubble gum in my mouth.

I didn't dare keep chomping away on that gum, so I quickly lifted my arm to my mouth and stuck it on the leather of my hand splint.

I positioned myself in front of the microphone, forgot about the gum, smiled at the congregation, breathed a quick prayer, and started speaking.

Toward the middle of my message, I got excited about a favorite Bible verse. With exaggerated gestures, I emphasized each point.

After a few minutes I heard giggles . . . then muffled laughter on the second row.

I looked at my lap and, to my horror, the wad of gum was stuck to everything—the arm of my wheelchair, my slacks, and my sweater. With all that gesturing I had woven an incredible web of bubble gum all over the front of me. Somehow the gum had even attached itself to the microphone stand. I was mortified!

There was no way I could continue. I laughed a bit disconcertedly with the crowd while a kind soul from the first row came and untangled me.

At that point my message changed to something about the friends of Lazarus unraveling him from his web of graveclothes. Needless to say, it was pretty hard to get back to the serious message I had prepared.

We all have those days. So keep your sense of humor. Because you are more removed from the situation than your handicapped friend, you can have a real part in making those "mountains into molehills." Perhaps it's on those days that you can put Galatians 6:9 to the test: "Let us not become weary in doing good, for at the proper time we will reap a harvest if we do not give up."

If it means cleaning up extra messes, taking more time to fix a flat on a wheelchair, having to interrupt your day to do unexpected errands—whatever it takes—you can help lighten the day for your friend. You may even laugh about it tomorrow.

If you don't want to be weary in doing good today, then you need to have a sense of humor. No one likes to feel like they're a burden. And by keeping a sense of humor while you help your disabled friend, you'll elevate your service to a joy. And that's a long way from making your friend feel like a millstone around your neck.

Adaptive equipment

Many physically-handicapped people must use wheelchairs. Others use walkers, canes, or crutches. This adaptive equipment, as it's called, does not restrict physically disabled people. In fact, for me, a wheelchair liberates me to move about more freely. I wouldn't say I am *confined* to a wheelchair. My chair is not a lifelong sentence to some sort of mobile prison, but a handy way of getting from one place to another. And with my power chair, I can get there by myself!

Occasionally I encounter a few architectural barriers when I'm scooting around. If it's a matter of a few steps, friends can lift my wheelchair. But not so with a flight of stairs. There have been many times when several men have wanted to carry me up a whole flight, but I've politely declined. Once I fell down a whole flight of stairs. And that did it for the old "love lifted me" routine.

So don't be offended if the person in a wheelchair rejects your offers to take the place of an elevator. Respect his wishes.

Understand that his wheelchair is a heavy item, even without the added body weight. Your disabled friend may be genuinely concerned about hurting your back. In fact, I still struggle with guilt feelings when I think of a good friend of mine who still has back problems from lifting me nearly five years ago.

Muscular dystrophy

If you've ever seen a Jerry Lewis muscular dystrophy telethon, then you have a good idea of what MD is all about. Pictures of little children in leg braces may tug at your heart strings, but you need some head knowledge also.

What are the facts? Muscular dystrophy hits kids. It is a disease. One third of the 200,000 people in the United States who have this disease are between the ages of three and thirteen.

For the families of these young people, the reminder of muscular dystrophy is more than a special television feature on a holiday weekend. It is the day-in, day-out presence of a degenerative disease. While muscles have a normal appearance, they gradually weaken and the rate of progression is often rapid with no remission.

MD itself is not fatal. However, eventually all the voluntary muscles are affected. When they are too wasted to perform their functions in circulation and respiration, death results.

You can imagine the emotional and physical trauma that friends and families experience as they watch their loved one weaken. Your support is crucial. They need shoulders to cry on and hands to help. They need time away for refreshment and reminders that they are loved.

During the progression of this disease, the person will become disabled, requiring crutches, and then a wheelchair. Eventually they will be confined to bed. With this additional care, you may find yourself ministering more to the family than the young person who has MD. Remember, ministry may entail simple tasks like mowing the lawn, praying, bringing in meals, cleaning the house, reminding them of God's care, reading a book to the child, taking a brother or sister out for an ice cream cone . . . the possibilities of ways to help are unlimited.

Multiple sclerosis

Perhaps the most fickle disease that results in physical handicaps is multiple sclerosis. A quarter to a half million people in the United States alone have this neurological disease of the brain and spinal cord.

In multiple sclerosis, a substance called myelin, which insulates the nerve fibers, hardens and is replaced by scar tissue. When the brain attempts to send messages to various parts of the body, the scar tissue distorts or blocks the impulses which control such functions as walking, talking, vision, etc.

Most frequently, multiple sclerosis will strike an adult of either sex between 20 and 40. The disease may begin with a single relatively minor symptom such as blurred vision in one eye, or weakness of a single limb. The symptom can disappear and no new warning signs show up for weeks, months, or even years. Other times, multiple sclerosis begins as an acute, incapacitating illness that progresses rapidly downhill.

That's why it's so difficult to deal with MS. It's capricious. For a period of time a person with multiple sclerosis may not be able to write or tie her shoes or even feed herself. Then in a matter of weeks or months she may regain the ability to do those things.

You can imagine how having this disease is like riding an emotional rollercoaster. The uncertainty is probably the hardest part. An ex-athlete not knowing whether he will be able to walk without a cane next month. The uncertainty of a young mother in deciding if she should hire extra help for the children. An executive in his 40's wondering if he should order a specially-equipped van as the transfers into his sedan become more difficult.

The emotional drain of dealing with multiple sclerosis only makes these decisions more difficult. According to my friend Bonnie, who has multiple sclerosis, "Fatigue is the second hardest factor MS'ers encounter. We need our friends to be flexible and to understand if we have a last-minute necessity to cancel, without being afraid of being excluded next time."

When I think of the best ways to help my friends who have MS, I think of the importance of providing emotional stability for them. I want to be a balanced resting place in their up and down world. And in that fluctuating world, the best comfort is found in Ecclesiastes 3:1–8. The Bible accurately describes those times of "ups" and "downs."

There is a time for everything,
and a season for every activity under heaven:
a time to be born and a time to die,
a time to plant and a time to uproot,
a time to kill and a time to heal,
a time to tear down and a time to build,
a time to weep and a time to laugh,
a time to mourn and a time to dance,
a time to scatter stones and a time to gather them,
a time to embrace and a time to refrain,
a time to search and a time to give up,
a time to keep and a time to throw away,

a time to tear and a time to mend,
a time to be silent and a time to speak,
a time to love and a time to hate,
a time for war and a time for peace.

And there is a time to help your disabled friend . . . perhaps it's now.

Head trauma

Before I leave physical disabilities I should talk about one that is a "first cousin" to spinal cord injury. Although its symptoms are many and varied, it is known under the general category of head injury. Similar to SCI, it usually affects young, vigorous people who are injured in a sports accident or automobile mishap.

Its symptoms may include blindness, paralysis, loss of memory, and impairment of mental function. Every year there are more than 140,000 people in the United States who die as a result of head injuries. Most of these deaths are directly the result of auto, motorcycle, or diving accidents. It would be an even higher number if not for modern medical techniques which save the lives of almost half that number. However, often those 50,000–70,000 are left permanently disabled by brain damage. Modern miracles of medicine have saved them, but we are lagging far behind in helping them.

It is no wonder that head injuries, and the resulting permanent impairments, are often called the "Silent

Epidemic." Oftentimes, someone who has been through this trauma will remain in a coma for several months before even regaining consciousness.

It is common that people with head injuries may not have the concentration or memory they once had and may not be able to control their emotions. Awareness of this epidemic will help us to reach out more sensitively to this misunderstood group of disabled persons.

Other physically-handicapping conditions

It would take volumes of medical textbooks to discuss every physically-handicapping condition. I've merely touched on a few. More could be said about environmental illness, Alzheimer's, Fredrick's Ataxia, spina bifida, post-polio syndrome, and many others. Be informed. Brush up on the facts surrounding the disability of your friend. If you'd like to learn more, visit your local library.

I must add one thought about what I believe is the most misunderstood disabling condition—cerebral palsy.

Cerebral palsy is a condition due to either damage or faulty development of the motor controls of the brain. The injury occurs before or during birth. Sometimes the damage happens early in a youngster's life. CP is not degenerative. It may be mild spasticity and speech impairment, or it may be so severe that the individual needs to be strapped tightly into his wheelchair.

Why is so much social stigma attached to cerebral palsy? Perhaps fear and ignorance play a large role. As I've shared before, people will wrongly assume that an individual is mentally retarded if he sits in a wheelchair, is spastic, or cannot speak. Don't chalk up people with CP as mentally handicapped simply because they may shuffle their feet when they walk or drool when they eat.

True, some people with cerebral palsy may be retarded due to the brain damage. But don't assume the worst. Susie, my friend with CP, has a master's degree from a nearby seminary. John, another friend who communicates with a wordboard, is a published poet.

Communicate with someone who has cerebral palsy, and you will quickly see beyond the uncontrolled actions into the heart of one made in the image of God.

Mental Handicaps

A mother stormed up to one of the elders in our church, tugging her young son alongside. By the look on her face, you could tell she was about to explode.

Pointing her finger at the elder, she stated her complaint. "I will not have my son participating in the same classroom with those idiots. For all I know, one of them will attack my son. Those mentally-retarded children are totally unpredictable and dangerous. I'm taking my son elsewhere."

With that, she turned on her heels and led her son away.

This scenario is not all that uncommon. It is repeated in churches everywhere. People fear the mentally retarded. There are many misconceptions and distortions and, unfortunately, the young people who are retarded are the ones who suffer most.

The irate mother in church was perhaps confusing mental retardation with mental illness. The truth is, retardation is not an illness. The two are quite separate. Let me explain.

Mental illness

Mental illness is just that—an illness. It is sometimes caused by chemical imbalances. Often it results from deep-seated psychological problems. As an illness, it can be treated with medication, surgery, or counseling. Mental illness doesn't necessarily interfere with intellectual abilities. Often it is earmarked by irrational behavior and sometimes violence.

Mental retardation

On the other hand, *mental retardation* occurs at or near birth and is characterized by impaired intellectual development. Mental retardation cannot be cured but can be treated through educational techniques, medication, or therapy. It is usually a lifelong condition. With understanding and patience, people who are mentally retarded are as giving, loving, and generous as the best of us.

You may run across labels such as PMR (profoundly mentally retarded), TMR (trainable mentally retarded), or EMR (educable mentally retarded). Some families dislike these labels, fearful that they compartmentalize too rigidly their mentally-handicapped children. Educators, however, use such labels in more accurately assessing the mental capabilities of children with whom they work.

Society has taken some real steps forward in helping

people who are mentally retarded. Personally, I believe there are more services, agencies, family counseling opportunities, and other helps for the mentally retarded than most people are aware of. But, oh, the bureaucracy of red tape that exists! You or your church can serve as an advocate for someone who is mentally retarded, helping him locate the available resources.

On another personal note, I am especially blessed whenever I have a chance to spend time with mentally-retarded friends—friends who are sometimes affectionately called "forever children."

Jesus, who spent so much time with children, blessing and calling them His own, should be our example. Even wise, mature saints are to exhibit the faith and trust of children, "for of such," He said, "is the kingdom of heaven."

Let me tell you about Rodney. Like a lot of the young fellows in our church, Rodney has really gotten involved. An active participant in church, he is often seen passing out bulletins at the front door before the Sunday morning service. Often Rodney will be running an errand to help his friend, a busy elder.

People like Rodney. He smiles a lot, lifting the spirits of those who come in contact with him.

But there is more to Rodney than just a helpful spirit. He is mentally retarded. He struggles with the ups and downs of being a teenager with a severe disability. He has known abuses and barriers as he has watched people keep a polite distance. Other kids go out on dates or drive cars. He has sat in the stands, watching his friends lead cheers and play football. He's played the role of a wallflower, observing his classmates at high-school dances.

Yet Christ has given Rodney a deep sense of peace. He knows he is different. He understands he will never be quite like his friends in the college and career department. Still he knows that God loves him. That is because there are folks at church who express God's unconditional love every time they chat with Rodney, or smile in return when he hands them a church bulletin.

What about these "forever children"? Do we want them relegated to a back room so we won't have to give any explanation for their behavior? Do we want their Sunday school class in the farthest corner of the church building— perhaps even with its own entrance— so they won't "offend" any visitors? We must remember they are as much a part of the family of God as the eldest and wisest of us. They leave us an example. For of such really is the kingdom of heaven.

Visual Impairments

Remember when you played hide-n-seek? You would turn out the lights and make yourself as small as possible behind a piece of furniture. Every once in awhile you'd hear a snicker as the person who was "it" came near. When it was your turn to be "it," suddenly you couldn't remember the exact placement of the furniture. Bruises appeared on your shins the next day to show for it!

It wouldn't be a bad idea to play that game once in a while even as adults. It might increase our sensitivity to those who have visual impairments, making us more aware of their particular needs. It's easy to take our eyesight for granted.

That fact is becoming reality to me. I've been painting a lot lately at my easel. The studio is a mess. Tracing paper is all over the floor, I've got watercolor stains on my clothes, and I can never find my good erasers. But despite all that, I love the time I spend at my easel.

It's that love which is getting me into trouble. You see, I get carried away and paint for hours. Before you know it, my neck gets a cramp and I notice my jaw aches from clamping so hard on the brush.

But what I really notice is my eyes. They never used to bother me. But this year it has begun to dawn on me that my eyes are not what they used to be. After even one hour at my easel, I've noticed that objects at a distance are getting blurry.

I have new prescription glasses. And in months to come I'll have to be more careful to rest my eyes every twenty minutes or so. Good clear eyesight is precious and worth every precautionary measure.

1.7 million people in the United States have severe visual impairments. That statistic reminds us to be thankful for the gift of sight. But more than that, we should be informed about how we can most naturally relate to someone who is visually impaired. The National Federation of the Blind has put out some courtesy rules to remember when meeting someone who is blind.

First, as with anyone who has a disability, please remember that blind folks are ordinary people. You don't need to raise your voice or address them as though they were children. Rather, talk to them as you would anyone else. Be certain to direct the questions to the person who is blind, rather than to his spouse or friend who is with him.

If a blind person is walking with you, don't grab his arm. Instead let him take your elbow if he chooses. Usually blind people will keep a half step behind you to anticipate curbs and steps.

If you know there is a blind person present when you walk into a room, speak as you enter. Introduce the blind person to others. Mention if there is a dog or a cat in the room. The possibility of a furry (albeit friendly!) creature springing into their lap is a very real one.

A partially-opened door to a cabinet, a room, or a car can be a hazard to somebody who is blind. Be aware of situations which could cause accidents.

There is no need to panic the first time you eat with a visually-impaired person. Blind people will not have trouble with ordinary table skills. But you may want to ask if they need "directions" regarding where bowls of food are placed. If food is already on their plate, describe where things are as on the face of a clock, such as, "The mashed potatoes are at two o'clock and the peas and carrots are at three." Blind people know their way around. Most will tell you if they need more assistance.

There's no need to avoid words like "look" or "see." Blind people use those words too. Last week I had a conversation that went like this . . .

"Hi, it's nice to see you," I said to the blind woman who signed up for our luncheon.

"Nice to see you too," she replied extending her hand.

I reached forward until my fingers touched hers. Immediately she gave me a handshake. "It's a beautiful morning, isn't it?" I said, glancing out the restaurant window at the trees and flowers. "Has anyone described the view to you yet?"

"Not actually. What's going on outside?"

"There's a row of oleanders by the window and . . . yes, I even see a few birds making a nest."

"Really!" she exclaimed.

Before I knew it, the rest of the people seated at the table joined in our lively conversation.

The senses of smell, touch, or hearing do not improve when a person becomes blind. It is just that the blind person relies on these senses more. Therefore, they may receive more information through those senses than most people. They can, as they put it, "feel" someone next to them. Blind individuals can "hear" a wall in front of them. They can sometimes "smell" someone coming down the street!

If a blind person is your house guest, show him around

the house as you would anyone. Don't forget the light switch. A blind person likes to know whether the lights are on or off.

People who are blind are willing to discuss their disability with you if you're curious. But it's mostly an old story to them. As was already shared, remember to talk about other topics and issues.

Let's crack some stereotypes. May I tell you about my friend, Amy? She is a young, pretty girl who graduated from college. She is also totally blind. Amy makes her way with a cane, preferring not to use a seeing eye dog. (She explains that, for her, it is too much bother to care for, feed, and exercise a dog.)

Amy loves bright and pretty colors in her clothes. She dresses with flair. She organizes her closets so that she doesn't confuse plaids with polka dots, bright pinks with muted greens. Many of the clothes she wears she has sewn herself.

This active, outgoing friend of mine loves God's Word. She reads the Bible in Braille and when she wants to highlight a certain verse, she will staple it. How's that for creativity?

Amy's story reminds me of an illustration my pastor shared at church. It had to do with a young blind girl who had met the Lord and had fallen in love with His Word. Much like Amy, she read Braille. In fact, this girl read so much that she developed callouses on her fingertips.

When she could no longer "read" because of the callouses, she began peeling them back to expose more sensitive tissue under the skin. Unfortunately, the raw and sore skin became permanently damaged and she could no longer read the Braille pages of her Bible.

Sadly, she had to part with her Braille Bible. So lifting the bulky manuscript to her lips, to kiss it goodbye, she discovered that she could "feel." Her lips picked up the various Braille indentations. She had found a new way to keep in touch with God's Word.

When I hear stories like this, or think of my friend Amy, it seems my disability isn't that big a deal. I can read God's Word. Although my fingers can't turn pages, I'm able to nudge a page by mouthstick. Whether with lips or a mouthstick, it can be done!

Hearing Impairments
Ever wonder which disability, blindness or deafness, would be the most difficult to deal with?

Helen Keller, both deaf and blind, answered that question. "Blindness separates you from things. But deafness separates you from people."

That quote took on new meaning for me a few years ago. My friends who are hearing impaired had told me that one of the greatest difficulties the deaf deal with is paranoia. Picture it. A deaf person is with a group of people with whom he can't communicate. He sees them gesture, he watches them laugh, he looks at their lips move. He may think he's missing out on the fun, or he may think he's the object of a joke.

I can almost identify! Ken and I were in Switzerland

to speak at a few meetings. Several German-speaking Swiss people escorted us as we journeyed from town to town. They were delightful folks and their English was good, but most of the time they enjoyed conversing together in their native tongue. I tried to pick up meaning from their sentences but it was impossible. At the dinner table I watched them chatter, gesture, and giggle. Occasionally they would look in our direction and warmly smile.

No doubt, these Swiss friends were having a grand conversation about positive things . . . the results of the meetings, people who had accepted Christ, the disabled who attended the crusade.

But, frankly, I kept fighting off the same paranoia that deaf people so often feel. I watched them, trying hard to understand, yet to no avail. Ken and I longed to be involved in their conversation. At times, I thought they were talking about us.

Because I experienced a real communication barrier myself, I can better appreciate what deaf people go through.

Since then, I've picked up pointers that will be useful as you reach out to somebody who is hearing impaired or deaf.

First, definitions can be confusing. A person who is *profoundly deaf* is one for whom the sense of hearing is nonfunctional for ordinary purposes of life, particularly for understanding speech. On the other hand, someone who is *hard of hearing* may have a defective sense of hearing, but can still hear and understand speech, especially with the help of a hearing aid and visual cues.

It's unwise to use phrases like "deaf mute" or "deaf and dumb." (Better to say, "My friend is deaf and doesn't speak.") It is like using the words "cripple" or "invalid." Those words carry negative connotations. Instead, use appropriate words like "deaf," "hard of hearing," or "hearing impaired."

People who are deaf are not mentally retarded. They have normal intellectual capabilities. However, they may lag behind academically because of the language barrier. You can imagine trying to learn a foreign language from somebody who is standing on the other side of a sound-proof glass—especially if the two of you have no language in common! Difficult? That's often what it's like for a deaf child to learn English.

Don't be afraid to talk directly to your deaf friend. Even if you need an interpreter to communicate, look at the deaf person as you talk. Doing this lets him know that you want to get to know *him,* not necessarily the interpreter whose hands you must "borrow." (Don't even ask the interpreter, "Would you ask him his name?"—the deaf person may surprise you and read your lips!)

Often there won't be an interpreter around to help you. For such times, it's good to learn some sign language. Deaf people will appreciate your effort. Also, keep a notepad and pencil handy to write messages. Planning ahead shows your desire to communicate.

Sometimes deaf persons have the ability to use their

voices. Most deaf individuals prefer not to do so, though, because of the poor quality of their speech. But if some-body is trying to communicate and you don't understand what he's saying, never pretend that you do. Instead, ask the person to repeat what he said or to write it down on paper. Remember, he's probably used to repeating. Also, encourage him to ask *you* to repeat if he doesn't catch what you are saying.

Some more hints? If you're aware that the hard-of-hear-ing person has a better ear, stand or sit on that side. They will be able to hear much better, too, if you cut down on the background noise.

Speak clearly, naturally, and at a moderate pace. It won't help to yell or exaggerate—you may be harder to understand! Both of these often result in distortion of speech.

Don't cover your face with your hands or objects. Many deaf people rely totally or partially on lip reading. So remember not to talk too fast.

Not long ago I was invited to speak at a church made up entirely of deaf and hearing-impaired people. As I talked from the platform, I noticed the pastor stood very close to me as he signed. In fact, his hands were right near my face. I learned later that he wanted to keep his hands near me so the deaf individuals in his congregation could read my facial expressions, and watch his interpre-tation at the same time.

I spied an elderly gentleman in the crowd who had his back to me. He was crouched over the hands of a young man who was facing me, his eyes intently fixed on my lips, glancing every once in awhile at the pastor's interpretation. I noticed the older man hardly moved at all and seemed to crouch closer to his friend's hands when I was sharing an interesting point.

After I finished speaking, I learned that the man was not only deaf, but also blind. Since he could not see the pastor's interpretations or see my lips, he depended on the expert signing of the young man. His hands, aged and wrinkled, were cupped around the fingers which gave him my message. Crouched close, he felt every single letter.

Curiously, the pastor mentioned to me that his deaf congregation considered the man to be the one who was *really* handicapped. He was hoping his congregation would be stimulated to reach out to meet the needs of people like the deaf-blind man.

Even disabled people need awareness!

How is your comfort level?

Can you see how getting your information straight can improve your comfort level? And if you don't know the facts, just ask.

I've thrown a lot of them at you in this chapter. Yet if

you still are uncomfortable with the idea of reaching out to a person whose disability you can't even pronounce, consider this.

If the worst thing you ever experienced was a month-long bout with the flu, you, no doubt, received comfort from God. Well, then, you can pass on the godly comfort you experienced to the young man with osteogenesis imperfecta.

2 Corinthians 1:4 says that God comforts us in all our troubles so that we can comfort others in *any* trouble.

That means *any* disability.

4
...How I Can Be
on the Giving End

Remember a morning when you just wanted to stay in bed?

For me, Sundays are tough. In fact, last Sunday I had to bring my emotions firmly in line with my will just so I could face the morning.

By the time Ken and I arrived at church and settled in, I was looking forward to the service. As the choir sang the opening hymn, one of the ushers wheeled in a young man from a local nursing home. He was new to church. The usher parked his wheelchair directly in front of me. The young man's arms were very spastic as he tried to hold onto the hymnal, and I wished someone in the pew would slide over to help.

My eyes were drawn to the back of his chair where a word board dangled from one of the handles. It was lop-sided, but I could read a few of the sentences on the board. A block of sentences was grouped together, listing weekly activities:

Please take me to therapy
Please wheel me to the lunch room
Please take me to occupational therapy
I need to see a nurse
I need to go to the bathroom

This was how the man communicated with his friends during the course of the week. He would obviously point to the particular sentence which best expressed his need.

Another list seemed to be for weekend routines. I was struck by the last sentence . . .

Please let me have a pizza
I want to go out to a ballgame
Please take me to a movie
Please take me to church

Here's the point. I'm sure that disabled man faces his share of Sunday mornings when he doesn't feel like getting up. Yet despite the difficulties of finding a staff person in the nursing home to help him arise extra early, he still wanted to be in church. It heartened me to picture him pointing to a sentence scrawled on a word board that said, "Please take me to church."

At that point my emotions immediately lined themselves up with my will. Suddenly I was happy. I was happy to be in church and fellowshipping with this young man who said, "Please . . . please take me to church."

He couldn't have realized how the Lord used him to encourage me. By his mere presence, my attitude had changed from a "grit-my-teeth-and-bear-it" stance to one of heartfelt joy and praise to God. Without realizing it, he was demonstrating the biblical injunction from 1 Thessalonians 5:11 to "encourage one another and build each other up."

Making the Disabled Feel Welcome

I once asked Dr. J.I. Packer, an outstanding theologian and author, what advice he might give to a Christian disabled person who was relegated to a back bedroom, away from Christian friends. What value does such a person have in the kingdom of Christ?

His answer would give worth even to the most severely disabled individual. "God doesn't want us for the sake of the things we can do for Him. He wants our love. He wants our fellowship. He wants our worship. And any of us—rich or poor, healthy or ill—can offer Him this."

The disabled are particularly aware of being judged by their abilities and accomplishments . . . or lack of them. It is in God's economy that the disabled person finds acceptance and love just because of *who he is,* not because of *what he can do*.

The church is to be a reality of that approval. Perhaps that's why we're told in Hebrews, "Let us not give up meeting together, as some are in the habit of doing, but let us encourage one another." There are no exceptions. We are all to come together, able-bodied and disabled alike.

No one is to be set apart. As much as possible, a handicapped person should have the opportunity to get involved with able-bodied people, to share, to worship with them. Sitting side-by-side in pews, their voices can unite in praise.

"Special sections" off to the side for people in wheel-chairs may tend to foster even more separation. (Even a section for the deaf can be more centrally located near the front of the church so the pastor's expressions are more visible.) It should be added, though, that some mentally-retarded individuals may appreciate a worship service of their own, better designed to meet their interest level and attention span.

But the rule of thumb should be involvement. Singing together, sitting near one another, touching, and being face to face has a way of breaking down barriers of fear and ignorance. Being one. That's what the body of Christ is all about.

I often refer to 1 Corinthians 12:14–23 when I encourage integration among the able-bodied and disabled. "Now the body is not made up of one part but of many . . . God has arranged the parts in the body, every one of them, just as he wanted them to be . . . The eye cannot say to the hand, 'I don't need you!' And the head cannot say to the feet, 'I don't need you!' On the contrary, those parts of the body that seem to be weaker are indispensable, and the parts that we think are less honorable we treat with special honor."

Do we honestly see the disabled as indispensable in our church?

Let me share a personal illustration. My hands, though paralyzed and without feeling, are indispensable to me. They are definitely the weakest members of my body. That's hard for some people to understand because they see photographs of me gesturing. It appears that I'm using my hands.

It sure looks like that, but let me explain. I have very strong shoulder muscles and fairly strong biceps. With those muscles I can flail my arms around. That makes my fingers and hands flop about. But I have absolutely no muscles from my elbows down. It only looks like I do.

Yet although my hands and fingers are lifeless, they are not useless. With the aid of a special arm splint I'm able to feed myself. When I drive, my hand rests in a handcuff attached to the steering column so I can brake and accelerate. My fingers can't turn pages, but with upper muscles I'm able to nudge them underneath a page and flip it over.

My hands and fingers, though lifeless and paralyzed, are so very useful!

Do you see the parallel? In that same chapter of 1 Corinthians it says, "Now you are the body of Christ and each one of you has a part in it" (v. 27). That includes your disabled friend—who, by the world's standards, seems so ineffective, totally unable to accomplish any real good for the rest of the fellowship.

It isn't that way. God says the weaker members are indispensable. The Body is not complete without them. And with a bit of creativity and help from the stronger members of the fellowship, they can make a difference . . . and they do.

I wish all churches viewed disabled people that way. Yet statistics show there are more than 30 million disabled people living in the United States, and 95% of the churches do not have a regular ministry that reaches out to them.

We can change that statistic! As the disabled are accepted into Christ's church, they will want to become actively involved. Here are a few practical ways we can help handicapped people feel welcome, as suggested by the Christian League for the Handicapped.

Get acquainted with at least one handicapped person in your church. That means more than a "Good morning . . . nice to see you . . . have a nice day." Spend an extended period of time with him during the week. Although it's important, Sunday morning conversation is often too hurried and interrupted to be more than superficial.

Be aware of families with disabled children. It may be

difficult for the parents to find experienced babysitters, and they, too, need an evening out now and then. Offer your services.

Sit next to a blind person or somebody with cerebral palsy. Offer to hold a hymnbook or look up Bible passages for them.

Suggest to your Bible study group to take on a love project for a handicapped individual. Rake a lawn, do minor repair jobs, or wash windows for a disabled homeowner in the neighborhood.

Acts of kindness such as these will pave the way for your disabled friend to become more involved in church.

Making Your Church Ready

The first preparation? Can your physically-disabled friend even get through your church door? If not, it could be a little embarrassing.

I'll never forget the time I went shopping at a local mall with a couple of my friends. In one of the stores we found a pile of pretty sweaters on a clearance table. We wanted to try on a few items so we grabbed the sweaters and headed for the ladies' dressing room.

I maneuvered my power wheelchair through the door of the dressing room. Before I knew it, I was stuck in the narrow aisle. I couldn't inch forward or backward.

Worse yet, a lot of other women in the dressing room got stuck, too. I was blocking them in. There was no way for them to get out, save climbing over me. And they weren't the type of ladies to do that. There I sat, unable to say anything cute and clever. I felt horrible—the women probably had schedules to meet and appointments to keep.

What a traffic hazard. The manager, along with the store clerk, pushed and pulled my wheelchair until finally it unwedged. I was embarrassed. (The manager was even more embarrassed. He promised to make room for wheelchairs!) I learned an important lesson, too. Always check the accessibility of any dressing room before I agree to try on clothes!

I giggle when I think of that incident. But I wasn't giggling when it happened. These situations happen to the disabled more than any of us would think.

Thankfully, more is being done all the time to remove many of the architectural barriers that have existed over the years. Many architects of public buildings and malls have planned their structures with a new awareness for the handicapped.

Unfortunately, the church has lagged behind in providing accessibility. So double-check your church building. If there are too many architectural roadblocks to overcome, your friend may feel like her presence just isn't all that important to the church.

Accessibility means far more than wide doorways and ramps. See your church through the eyes of a disabled person. Are you truly putting out "welcome" signs? Are you getting the message across, "Hello! Come on in! We've prepared a place for you and we want you to feel right at home"?

No doubt your church already has some welcome signs.

Ringing bells and open doors, smiling ushers and firm handshakes are a great start.

But there are other creative ways to welcome the disabled. A close and designated parking area for people in wheelchairs says "welcome" loudly and clearly. A curb cut will communicate, "We've taken the time to think ahead. We've done something about these obstacles to make it easier for you to fellowship here."

Walk through your church building with a physically-handicapped friend. Take notes as he points out possible changes that would make it easier to get around. Lowered water fountains. Bathrooms with wide alcoves and grab bars. A portion of a pew removed so a wheelchair does not block an aisle. Blocks of wood which can be wedged under the front wheels of a chair that is parked on a slant.

Making a church accessible is not easy. And it can be expensive. But we're not talking about making major structural changes immediately. The important thing is that you lay out the "welcome mat," at least making it possible for a wheelchair to get from the parking lot to the sanctuary without having to be carried up a flight of stairs.

The hearing impaired could use amplifying devices which can be hooked into several pews. Is there sufficient lighting in the sanctuary for the hearing impaired? It is difficult for them to read lips or to see signing if the lighting is poor. If your church has a ministry with hearing impaired, consider installing a TDD (telecommunication device for the deaf) so they can call the church.

The visually impaired will know they are welcomed when they see large-print hymnbooks and Bibles. And what a vital ministry for the blind if someone would Braille the hymns and the sermon text each week. There's no doubt about that welcome!

Even more important than these architectural welcome mats is the attitude of God's people. Jesus understood this. In Luke 14 He told the story of a man who had a great banquet and invited many guests. Now it's hard to imagine, but these friends found excuses to do anything but eat! They had fields to attend to, oxen to try out, and a new wife—maybe good excuses, but it angered the master that other things were more important to them than his banquet. So he ordered the servant, "Go out quickly into the streets and alleys of the town and bring in the poor, the crippled, the blind, and the lame . . . Go out to the roads and country lanes and make them come in, so that my house will be full."

Notice the insistence in the master's command—"bring them in" . . . "make them come in." Does your disabled friend sense this kind of urgency in your invitation to come to church? Or is it a kind of off-the-cuff, "Uh, by the way, uh, if you don't have anything better to do on Sunday, why don't you see if you can't come to church."

We're to bring them in, "make" them come. Now I'm not telling you to drag your disabled friend, against his will, to church next Sunday. Let me explain . . .

After living with the demands of a physical limitation

all week, most handicapped people are worn out by Sunday. They simply lack the emotional stamina, the initiative, to attend church. They spend Monday through Friday arranging attendant care, shopping, doctor visits, and housekeeping. The last thing they may want to do is ask one more person for a ride to church. It's easier to stay home and watch church on television.

Take my friend Debbie. She is in a wheelchair and has a speech impediment. She takes the bus during the week, but must find other transportation on Sundays. Every Saturday afternoon she would have to make the rounds of phoning different people for a ride. Her wheelchair eliminated drivers who have small, sporty cars. Then she had to cross off her list people with bad backs. And she also avoided asking people who had trouble accepting her deformities. She didn't want to make them ill at ease.

Now, my friend Debbie is a particularly persevering sort. But the truth is most disabled people will not dig in their heels and persevere when it comes to arranging their own transportation to church services. Although the people they ask usually have valid reasons for not providing rides, the average disabled person tends to interpret a "no" answer as a personal rejection.

Finding it difficult to get a ride to church suggests that they are unwanted. And once the disabled person feels rejected by a congregation, the next thought may be that God doesn't want disabled people either.

Our responsibility is clear. We must take the initiative

to get handicapped people to church. Invite, yes. But we must go beyond that. Like the story in Luke 14, we must *bring* them.

Evangelizing Your Disabled Friend

When I was in the hospital, I dreaded people who would come into my ward prepared to announce the gospel to me. And I don't use that word "announce" lightly. I'm sure they had a definite notion of how the conversation would go. Maybe some of those people assumed I would ask the standard questions. In their minds they had standard answers.

Looking back, I wish those conversations could have been more successful. One problem was that those people were more concerned about *imposing* their faith, rather than *exposing* it. Yet even now, years later, I fall into the same trap when I talk about Jesus to friends or neighbors who don't know Him. I impose rather than expose my faith.

Perhaps you've done the same. Jesus has made a difference in your life, and you're convinced He will do the same for your disabled friend. You mechanically recite salvation verses, praying all the while that you won't forget anything. But your friend seems unmoved. You can't help but be depressed by her rejection of Christ.

The truth is, we cannot make someone a Christian. We must let our faith be known, but we cannot dump it on others. In fact, if we aggressively throw our spiritual weight around, it could indicate our misunderstanding of the role of the Holy Spirit. We cannot convert anyone. Only the Spirit of Christ can do that.

That should give us comfort when it comes to giving the gospel to someone who, let's say, has just learned that his disability is permanent.

Forget imposing your faith on your disabled friend. To expose your faith is so much easier . . . and so much more natural. There is nothing threatening or intimidating about getting into an honest conversation about God and what He means to you. It can be winsome and persuasive to casually share the reality of God in your everyday life.

Openness is appealing. Don't be afraid to ask leading questions. And don't get defensive. You're not on the attack. You're simply opening up your life. You're letting another person see, in the most natural way, what makes you care, love, and give.

It can be intimidating to share Christ with someone who just broke her neck in an automobile accident, or a person whose disability is causing him further physical problems. In fact, this conversation happened very recently . . .

". . . And that's why I believe in God," I said as I leaned back in my wheelchair, letting my words sink into the thinking of the young man with post-polio syndrome. I didn't have to wait long.

"Don't talk to me about a good God. If He was so

good, He would have never let this happen to me." The tone of his voice was soft as though he sincerely did not understand.

It was a delicate moment, so I waited before responding. Finally, I continued, "Yeah, I know exactly how you feel. I've been there myself. Lying in a hospital bed with tubes running in and out of you tends to throw out of focus any preconceived notions of a good God. And from a human point of view, God certainly doesn't look very good, does He?"

The man looked a little stunned, surprised even. I had thrown back at him his hot-potato question. He didn't know what to do with his argument. I could tell he was wondering why I, a Christian, would agree with him that God doesn't look very fair. "Uh . . . no, he doesn't look fair . . . Listen, are you playing some sort of game?" he said, squinting his eyes.

"Not at all. I'm just being truthful. From an earthly point of view, God doesn't come out smelling like a rose when it comes to human suffering." I could tell the hot potato was cooling down a bit.

He looked me straight in the eyes, his expression more relaxed. As I watched the wheels turn in his head, I realized how explosive emotions dissipate when you deflect them with a little common sense.

Finally he spoke. "So . . . run by me one more time that stuff about a heavenly point of view."

From there on the discussion was no longer angry, but

sincerely earnest. I shared a heavenly, biblical perspective about his disability. It was his first step to eventually accepting Christ.

You may have to juggle a few hot-potato questions from your disabled friend—especially if he doesn't know Christ. Your friend will listen if you use careful common sense in handling God's Word.

These very people who have suffered are special objects of God's care and concern. In Revelation 3 Jesus says that He wishes people were either cold or hot. It grieves Him that so many are lukewarm about spiritual things. Most disabled people I know are definitely not lukewarm!

Heavy-duty suffering has a way of pressing people up against spiritual walls. They are either hot—that is, super interested in things in the Bible—or they are ice cold—calloused and indifferent toward a life in Christ.

But, look! Jesus says that's a good place to be.

So don't let fear or intimidation overcome you when faced with an opportunity to share the gospel with someone who is disabled. After all, the Spirit is probably doing double duty in the life of a person backed into spiritual corners. It is the Spirit who has prepared the other person's heart, and it is the Spirit who will give you the natural and supernatural words to say. It may be that you were brought into his life for such a time as this!

Being on the Giving End

After I left the hospital, finally drawing closer to Christ, I read 1 Corinthians 3:11–13, "For no one can lay any foundation other than the one already laid, which is Jesus Christ. If any man builds on this foundation using gold, silver, costly stones . . . his work will be shown for what it is." That hospital experience was God's way of laying my foundation bare. Now He was ready to begin the slow process of cementing into my character gold and silver. I had to learn to be a servant. I had to start to be on the giving end.

Eight long years passed and finally I was able to catalog my journey in the book *Joni*. I guess I would have been content, after the book came out, to remain on the farm and continue to paint. But opportunities kept coming: other books, chances to travel, a movie, a record. And God was building into my life a deeper love of Jesus and a desire to help others reach their full spiritual maturity in Christ.

Books and speaking engagements have little to do, though, with the silver and costly stones talked about in 1 Corinthians 3. Popularity and prestige carry little weight with God. For that matter, most disabled people don't have the chance to give their testimony at a Christian women's club, much less put it all down in a book. *But the success of what a disabled person builds on his foundation is measured by the gold of obedience, the silver of a refined faith, and the precious gems of loyalty and faithfulness as he serves others by exercising his unique spiritual gift.*

Disabled People Also Have Gifts!

1 Peter 4:10–11 says, "Each one should use whatever spiritual gift he has received to serve others, faithfully administering God's grace in its various forms. If anyone speaks, he should do it as one speaking the very words of God. If anyone serves, he should do it with the strength God provides, so that in all things God may be praised through Jesus Christ." This verse doesn't apply to only the able-bodied. It's for the disabled, too. We all have gifts of the Spirit.

May I encourage you to help your disabled friend discover his spiritual gift? Would you help him find a niche in your church where he can exercise his gift? For openers, look through the list of gifts in Romans 12:6–8. What area of service listed there gives your disabled friend the most joy? Encourage him to use his gift, praying for wisdom and direction. Perhaps he will find a place to serve where no one else is meeting the need. (Your church may have to accommodate the limitations of your disabled friend, forgetting how "things have always been done" in the past.)

Don't let the disability stand in the way of service. My friend, Bonnie, has MS and is in a wheelchair. She teaches a lively class of second graders. Those children learn about Jesus while gaining handicap awareness—all at the same time. And Bonnie's right at their eye level!

Team teaching is a good idea if your friend has the gift

of teaching yet has limitations. Results do not depend on how well a teacher passes out books, collects papers, or sharpens pencils. Your disabled friend can borrow someone's hands to do those tasks, while she devotes herself to teaching. The results, then, depend on the Spirit. 1 Corinthians 2:2–5 says, "For I resolved to know nothing while I was with you except Jesus Christ and him crucified. I came to you in weakness and fear, and with much trembling. My message and my preaching were not with wise and persuasive words, but with a demonstration of the Spirit's power, so that your faith might not rest on men's wisdom, but on God's power."

Kathleen M. Muldoon, in her "Finger, Toe and Lip Service," catalogued a number of ways that disabled Christians can exercise their gifts in the church. The list may give you other ideas on how the disabled in your congregation can use their Spirit-given spiritual gifts:

A ministry of prayer

There are often prayer chains, groups, or cells within the church. For the severely disabled person who may not be able to even leave his hospital bed or home, there can be a powerful ministry of prayer. He can intercede for the needs of his friends, family, and church. I know of a disabled person who is a personal prayer partner of a college and career pastor—he receives an updated list on the names and needs of young people in the church. When people in the congregation become aware of this ministry, there will be no lack of petitions!

Prayer can be an international ministry. The disabled person can pray for missionaries around the world and for religious and national leaders. It's no small task to pray for food for the starving, protection for the persecuted, and the many other petitions that the Spirit reminds him of as he hears the news of the world and nation.

A mail ministry

There's nothing like receiving a note of encouragement from someone. A mail ministry is one way to build others up in the faith, deepen friendships, encourage those who are ill, and share meaningful Scriptures.

You can assist your friend in a mail ministry by offering your hands if they are unable to write. Offer to operate a tape recorder for them as they "talk" a letter.

Disabled people can reach out to those that many others do not have time for. Think of prisoners who go months without receiving mail; people in convalescent homes who look for letters in their mailbox; people in hospitals who would appreciate a get-well card; or people in a rehab center who need a reminder that there are brighter days ahead. Most likely your pastor knows of shut-ins who have little contact with the outside world and would cherish a note. And missionaries spend much of their time writing letters and yet receive very few in return.

As with the prayer ministry, the Lord will bring to mind those that need this kind of encouragement. In these areas, the disabled can shine.

A telephone ministry

"Reach out and touch someone" is far more than just a catchy telephone ad. It's something that the disabled can do from their own homes for the good of the body of Christ. Many elderly people long for the opportunity to talk to someone—to know that there is someone who cares about them, who will ask about their family, who will allow them to reminisce. A telephone ministry may involve "checking up" on the needs of people who have little contact with others during the week.

A creative friend of Kathleen Muldoon has a ministry to children in her church. She put a note in the bulletin and asked parents to contact her if they were interested in her calling their children when they arrived home from school. What started as just a "check-in call" has developed into friendships with the children. They pray together. She even helps them with occasional problems. This disabled person is someone very special to each of those kids.

My friend Diane, who uses a handicap-adapted phone, is responsible to telephone disabled people who sign up for transportation to our church during the week. She's developed a network, linking drivers with people who need a ride.

The opportunities to minister, using the gifts God has given, are unlimited. God has made us each uniquely in His image. Our gifts are unique. And our opportunities to use those gifts in His kingdom are unique. That should make each one of us sense the urgency of serving Him—in our own way, in the place He has put us, using the gifts He has given us. It's an awesome privilege.

Happy serving!

There are ways that even the most severely disabled can serve the Lord and others in His church. Consider these . . .

The service of hiddenness
The service of small things
The service of guarding the reputation of others
The service of being served
The service of common courtesy
The service of hospitality
The service of listening
The service of hearing the burdens of each other
The service of sharing the Word of Life
—Richard J. Foster in *Celebration of Discipline*

5
Who Touched Me?

The crowd gathered quickly on that hot dusty afternoon in the town of Capernaum. The news was out about Jairus' daughter. Rumor had it that she was dying. But other news drew even more people—Jesus was in town.

Plunging through the crowd, Jairus ran, tripping over his feet. He didn't reach out to shake the hands of others as he so often had done. Rather, his eyes were fixed on the only Man who could help him.

The set of his face told all—Jairus had an urgent problem. His ruddy complexion had lost its color, and deep worry lines etched his face. People huddled, whispering as he pushed by them. Perhaps the rumors were true.

Maybe his daughter really was dying. Oh my, what the family must be going through! Many eyes watched as he talked to Jesus. Something was terribly wrong.

As Jesus turned to follow him, Jairus' face relaxed. They were on their way to his daughter. But how he wished for a quicker, easier route than to have to return through the pressing crowd.

They needed to get home quickly, but Jesus would not be rushed. People pulled his cloak and reached for his arms. How rude and insensitive. Why would they bother Him at a time like this? Suddenly something caused Him to stop.

I should say "someone" caused Him to stop. We don't even know her name, yet three of the gospel writers included her in the Scriptures. She was a woman with a special need. For twelve years she had bled, and repeated doctoring only resulted in poverty and worse health. We don't get the impression from Scripture that this lady had much to offer. She was not a leader like Jairus. Probably few, if any, people in the crowd recognized her. Not that she particularly wanted anyone to know who she was. It had become embarrassing to be in public. She didn't even feel like the same woman she once was. Those closest to her sadly remembered the vigorous woman they had known. She had once been beautiful, the envy of others as she cared for her family.

But the years of bleeding had taken their toll. Her quick movements had become halting and labored. A shawl covered her dull eyes. She was tired, so tired.

She did not have the confidence to push her way up to Jesus. But she saw Him coming her way. Perhaps He could do for her what many doctors couldn't. She rallied her strength, stretched, and touched the edge of His garment. She was sure He didn't even realize it.

And a touch changed a life.

Not only did she find the physical healing she so needed, but the Savior took time to stop, talk, and assure her of forgiveness.

A Touch in Passing

Read more about it in Mark 5:21–43. This story of Jesus gently restoring a desolate woman is a poignant parentheses in the middle of a triumphant narrative about the healing of Jairus' daughter. There is a marked contrast in these two miracles. On the one hand, Jesus changed the entire agenda for the day in order to visit the home of a dying child. But on the way, just in passing, Jesus took a moment for a woman. She was barely an acquaintance. But with a tender touch He changed her life.

How many lives do we touch each day?

Or perhaps a better question would be, how many lives *could* we touch each day? How often could we "stop on the way" to be kind to someone who needs a gentle touch?

There are so many ways this can be done. Let's think about the woman in the crowd that day. There are people like that everywhere we go. It could be the teenager in his wheelchair venturing out to shop for the first time since his injury. He used to stride through the same mall with his friends. Now he is back and all that has changed. He dreads seeing any of his friends because they seem so uncomfortable around him. He wishes things were the way they used to be.

Your touch could help the attractive lady sitting in the pew next to you on Sunday morning. It's been so long since anyone has reached out to her. She cares for her elderly father, and this is the only time during the week she can leave him. Yet even in the filled sanctuary she feels alone. Everyone seems too busy with other friends to get acquainted with her.

The blind man feels secure that he can get to work on the bus each morning, but why is it that no one ever strikes up a conversation with him? Oh sure, people don't ignore him if he asks questions of them. It's just that the casual camaraderie the other riders share doesn't quite extend to him. Are they afraid they will use words like "see" or "look"?

We pass people like these every day. Oftentimes we don't see them. Even less frequently do we touch them.

A Place to Start

So where do you start? You start at the easiest place. Begin with kindness and gentleness as Jesus did. Do the things that come the most naturally to you with your able-bodied friends.

A smile is a good place to start. What one of us doesn't like to be on the receiving end of a sincere smile? Like that advertisement about the "friendly skies," it makes us want to pass on the kindness that has been shown to us. How does that old saying go? "Smile and the whole world smiles with you."

Wise King Solomon knew that. In Proverbs he wrote, "A happy heart makes the face cheerful" and "A cheerful look brings joy to the heart." If we are going to be reaching out to the disabled with God's joy, it has to be translated from our hearts to the heart of the disabled friend. Here is the key—joy in our hearts is best demonstrated by our smiles, and that can bring joy to the hearts of others. It's not very profound, but it is a good beginning for any of us who want to show Jesus' love.

Sure you may be shy. Smiling at strangers (whether in wheelchairs or not) doesn't come easily. But you have to start somewhere. And like anything we feel uncomfortable with, it takes practice. Ask God for courage, then greet those around you with a smile—able-bodied and disabled alike. Start with family and good friends. Sometimes they are the ones who see your cheerful smile the least. As your smile becomes a more natural part of your conversation, then add it to your "thank you" to the paper boy or bank teller. With a little practice, a smile will come easily.

Like the verse in Proverbs says, "A word fitly spoken is as apples of gold" or as another translation puts it, "Like apples of gold in settings of silver is a word spoken in the right circumstances." We like it when people look us in the eye and talk to us. That cheery hello, a warm embrace, or a hug on the shoulder are as valuable as apples of gold. No price can be put on them. We are far richer for having given and received a smile and a good word.

Don't forget though—treat the disabled as you would any other person. If you are comfortable with smiling and greeting people in church, then smile and greet the deaf girl on the end of the pew. And wouldn't it make her day to have you learn the sign for "hello" or "good to see you"?

Incidentally, some people are hesitant about smiling and greeting those with disabilities for fear that the friendliness will be misconstrued as pity. Don't worry—your rule of thumb should be to greet disabled people as you would anyone else. But one word of caution: Disabled people have a way of seeing right through your motives. If you *do* foster pity, then prayerfully examine your own motives before reaching out to others. Pity—that condescending attitude that "feels sorry" for others—never helps anyone.

A Smile . . . and Then Some

The child in the wheelchair that you often see sitting in the front yard down the street would probably love to tell you about his pet or friends. Your question would be a touch he would not soon forget. And his answer would provide him the chance to be on the giving end.

I enjoy it when people greet me with smiles or even a question. I don't mind the honest curiosity that people often express about my adaptive equipment. For instance, I've had many people half stare and half smile at me in the supermarket parking lot while I'm using my mechanical lift to get into the van. In fact, a nicely dressed woman pushed her grocery cart to her Mercedes parked next to my van and stopped. She couldn't get to her driver's door until my lift had finished raising. I could tell she didn't want to stare, but she couldn't look away either.

Finally, she crossed her arms, smiled, and said, "I've always heard about these kind of vans and I've never seen one work. Do you mind if I watch?"

Now to me, *that* is staring of the nicest kind. And that is the sort of staring I don't mind. The woman did not have a morbid curiosity. She was honestly interested in the kind of equipment that makes independent living possible for me.

Looking at someone else with sincere interest may be acceptable—*if* you personalize your look with a greeting like, "Hi, I'm really interested in how you manage that wheelchair. Do you mind if I watch how you work your mechanical lift?" That's the kind of curiosity most people with disabilities don't mind.

Remember, though, to look past the gizmos, gadgets, and electrical wizardry. The equipment may be interesting, but the person using that equipment is far more deserving of your attention. He may need your kindness far more than your curiosity.

Some Practical Ways to Help an Acquaintance

Acquaintance. That seems like a cold word. But in this chapter we are not discussing how you can help those disabled people who are your close or intimate friends. An acquaintance may be someone you encounter in passing. Goodness—you may end up helping someone you don't even know, someone you've never met! Let me explain . . .

Just yesterday I was feeling really down. I can't explain it. I don't know why. Some days the everyday wear and tear of living life in a wheelchair is just plain hard.

A little card arrived on my desk with a handmade Bible bookmark in it. I looked at the address on the envelope. I didn't even know the woman who sent it. But the verse on the bookmark happened to be just the thought I needed to brighten my day.

In Titus 3:8 those of us who have trusted in God are told to be careful to devote ourselves to doing what is good. That's what this acquaintance did for me. The woman may not have known how to push a wheelchair or empty a leg bag, but she did one thing she knew how to do—she sent a word of encouragement.

That is a good example of how we can touch others with Jesus' kindness. Whether it is a casserole to help the mother of a retarded child, a ride to church for a young man with cerebral palsy, or a conversation with a teenager who is non-verbal—devoting ourselves to doing what is good just calls for us to reach out, as Jesus did, with gentleness and kindness.

It may be something simple like holding a shopping mall door open for a woman in a wheelchair. After all, you would do the same for an able-bodied woman juggling a shopping bag and a stroller.

So. Once you are comfortable sharing a smile and offering light words of encouragement, how can you help further?

The Next Step

Let's say there seem to be no disabled people in your community—or at least you don't know where they are. You rarely see a handicapped person at church. Even at the mall or grocery store, you don't even recall the last time you saw someone with a visible disability. You wonder if those statistics you read are really true of your neighborhood.

Your ideas will certainly change the minute you pick up the local Yellow Pages, and flip through to the names and addresses of a couple of nursing homes, convalescent centers, or hospitals. Talk to the chaplain, social service worker, or community services director and inquire if they have patients or clients who might want some letters written to their families with whom they have not been able to correspond. When I was in the hospital, I loved people like that who helped me with small things. It meant a great deal that volunteers sat down by my bedside with pen and paper in hand.

My mother would stand by my bedside for hours, holding a book for me to read. When she tired of standing, she sat and read to me. You could go one better—read a book together. Every week you might plan to read two or three chapters. Before you know it, you will both have the satisfaction of a completed story . . . and a friendship that goes beyond a mere acquaintance.

Here's a good one—how about taking some Windex or chrome cleaner and shining up somebody's wheelchair? A clean wheelchair isn't often at the top of a priority list of things to do. But just as you like your car clean, waxed, and shined, others like to have their wheelchairs looking great.

My cousin Eddie brought in record albums of environmental sounds. In that stuffy hospital room, we listened for hours to rustling leaves in the wind by a gurgling brook.

Bring in some notions from a pharmacy. Stationery might be useful, or dental floss, Q-tips, a hair brush, or lotion. Discover the person's interests and pick up a magazine he'd like. Can you imagine how good some Baskin-Robbins ice cream or a pizza would taste to someone who has been in a hospital for months?

Or maybe you can spend time listening.

Seemingly small expressions of love can make all the difference in the world. Acquaintances such as neighbors, kids from high school, or the church youth group can play an important role in the life of a disabled person.

If You Don't Reach Out, Who Will?

In this chapter we have talked about small and ordinary ways to reach out and touch the lives of the handicapped around us. Most of the things mentioned do not take much time or planning, but are just genuine deeds of kindness that we can do in passing, much as Jesus healed the woman with an issue of blood. They are deeds that do not ask for a lasting commitment. Rather, they are often a one-time action, yet with lasting results . . . perhaps even a changed life.

Jesus put a high value on kindness. I was challenged by that truth in a Bible study on the seven last statements spoken by Jesus from the cross.

As Jesus was slowly dying, He called out, "I am thirsty."

As others shared their thoughts on the verse, I tried to picture myself next to the cross. What would I do if I heard my Savior say He was thirsty? "You know," I began, "if I had been there that day, I would have raced for the nearest canteen. I would have grabbed a bucket or a hose or something. No sponge and vinegar. I would have done anything to get Him a drink of water. I mean, after all, this is Jesus who is thirsty, not my next-door neighbor or a kid down the street! This is Jesus who is asking for a glass of water."

Everyone agreed that they would have reacted the same way. Our entire Bible study group would have dug a well if we had to! Anything to get a drink to our Savior.

But then I made a curious comment. Why is it that we care little about the biblical mandate where Christ says, " 'I was thirsty and you gave me drink' . . . Then the righteous will answer Him, 'Lord, when did we ever give you a drink?' . . . and the King will reply, 'I tell you the truth, whatever you did for one of the least of these brothers of mine, you did for me' "?

Why is it those words of the Lord Jesus don't move us into action? There is not one of us who wouldn't have given Jesus a drink as He hung on that tree, but when it comes to the least of the brethren, we drag our feet. We sit back and reason that somebody else will take care of the need. Giving a drink to the least of His brethren doesn't carry the same sense of urgency. The thirst of "the least of these" simply doesn't match up to the thirst of our Savior.

But Jesus made it plain that when we meet the need of anyone, we clearly minister to Him personally. Helping even the least of these brethren is like serving Christ with our own hands. He will remember such deeds of kindness when we meet Him in eternity. On that Day, we may try to reason with Jesus, "Now, Lord, when did I ever see you thirsty? I mean, if I had been at the cross that day, I surely would have given you a drink."

And He will say in His gentle way, "The extent that you did it to one of the least of my brethren, you already did it unto Me."

Thinking back on the Bible story about the woman with the issue of blood, I'm glad that Jesus set an example for us. In His mind, she may have been one of the "least of the brethren." I get shivers thinking about the thoughtless, self-centered crowd around her, elbowing her out of the way to get a closer look at the Master.

Please. Don't look past the disabled people you may encounter as mere acquaintances. Be aware. Be sensitive. Don't assume that someone else will take care of the need. If it appears as though that disabled friend needs a hand, gladly give it, would you?

Ask yourself the question—how would you have responded to your thirsty Savior if you happened to pass by the cross that day?

6
Hey, Let's Go through the Roof!

How many of us like to be in a crowd where people shove, push, and elbow one another? It's worse when the crowd is trying to funnel through one gate or a door. If somebody tries to cut in front of you, there goes the lid on your temper, and you nudge him out of the way.

When I think of large crowds, I recall the Bible story about four friends who wanted to take their paralyzed buddy to see Jesus. Everyone was talking about the Master's last visit to their village. During that time, many had been miraculously healed. In fact, the centurion's servant had been raised up without Jesus even going to his house. The four friends remembered it well.

They also remembered that Jesus had confronted a man with an unclean spirit. Before their eyes Jesus dramatically cast out the demon, and the man was completely restored.

Once again, the village tongues were wagging—this same Jesus was back in town!

That's why the four friends arrived at the home of their paralyzed companion so early in the morning. They were going to take him to see Jesus. Today was the day that the Master would get their friend off his bed!

Perhaps they helped him dress. Fed him breakfast. Lifted him onto his cot. It seemed no effort to carry their buddy that morning—quite different from other times when they had no hope. Even the distance seemed short to the place where they knew Jesus was ministering. But as they drew closer, the crowd grew thicker. It seemed everyone else had the same idea—everybody in town wanted to witness the Master's miracles first-hand. It was one thing to hear about His healings, but quite another to see them.

But why did Jesus choose to teach and heal in an ordinary house? Why didn't He head for the synagogue where there would be more room? The house didn't have a front yard or balconies for a good view. There were no shade trees to escape the hot sun. In fact, the joy and expectancy of the crowd began to sour as the morning sun rose in the sky. The closeness became oppressive.

The four friends placed the paralyzed man on the ground and surveyed the scene. Most people in the crowd didn't even look sick, much less need the Healer, like their palsied friend. Yet everyone, rich and poor alike, seemed to have the same urgency about seeing Jesus.

They strained on tiptoe to catch a glance. How would they get through the crowd? They couldn't plan on coming back later. Who knew if Jesus would ever be back in town again? Their disabled friend must see the Master today. This called for creativity. An alternate plan of action.

They scratched their heads, thinking. Going through the door would not work. It was doubtful that anyone would clear the way for them. And once they got under the roof, what guarantee did they have that they could get close to Jesus at all?

That was it! The roof! That's all they needed to do—just get under the tiles on that roof. The effort would be a small price to pay if it meant their friend could be healed. Sure, they'd be happy to fix the roof afterward. And if they couldn't get the tools, they'd find someone else who could.

Becoming a Friend

As you read the account of this story in Mark 2:1–12, you see persistence pay off. A ripped-up roof certainly got Jesus' attention! The four friends—their faith, creativity, and commitment—probably drew more attention. No one could help but notice how the friends overcame an insurmountable hurdle to help the paralyzed man.

When Jesus healed the man, he took special note of the faith which the four exhibited—faith that was willing to stick its neck out, roll up its sleeves, and creatively do the job that needed to be done. Perhaps even Jesus thought of His own words, "whatever you did for one of the least of these brothers of mine, you did for me."

In this story we see a deeper relationship between a disabled person and his friends. Not just a touch or passing acquaintance, as we observed in the last chapter, but the development of a real friendship. A relationship in which friends share common interests and activities. A shared commitment of time and energy.

That's how friendships began for me when I was in the hospital. I was so thankful for friends who would come visit me. When they walked into the room, I desperately wanted them to draw closer.

But sometimes people would merely pull up their chairs and sit no nearer than the foot of my bed. Others, who came with them, would linger in the doorway, leaning against the wall. I assured them that the nurses wouldn't mind if they sat on my bed. But most of those people stayed at an arm's length—or maybe two arms' lengths—distance from my shoulders. I say "shoulders" because that's where I could have felt their embrace if only they had reached out.

That was hard to deal with back then. I felt thin and ugly and there were strange odors in that hospital. Nobody showed me a mirror for the longest time. The cautious and guarded reaction of some of those people who came into my room underscored to me that it was true—I *was* awful to look at.

They couldn't have known that their thoughtless reactions had such a negative impact on me. Rather, it would have been better to hear somebody use a little humor and honesty, saying forthrightly, "Joni, for being in this hospital as long as you have and for going through so much, you look halfway decent. I bet you're the best looking, totally paralyzed person in this hospital!" That sort of humor would have broken the tension.

Think about it. When you visit a disabled person, or a friend who is ill, can you greet them with a caring embrace? Do you touch them where they can feel it—even if leaning over the guardrail of the bed is awkward? Don't worry about talking over the specifics of an illness you know little about. Nobody is going to fall apart in front of you—or if they do, perhaps a good cry is exactly what they need.

Pull up a chair close to the head of the bed. If you share a special intimacy with your friend, ask to sit on the edge of the bed. Talk over a few interesting details of your day—don't assume she will feel sorry about the things she can't do. Ask her about a favorite memory. If it seems appropriate, encourage her to open up. Envision together the time of coming good health. (Or if your friend has a permanent disability, envision creative things you will do together—managing a wheelchair at the beach, adapting a canoe, or modifying a favorite campsite.)

Ask your friend if he would like you to bring in a favorite polo shirt from home. If your friend is a woman, flip through a hairstyle magazine. Discuss where you will go shopping together. Bring in a new embroidery pattern. Organize her old recipes into a box. Teach knitting or crocheting. Do crossword puzzles together. Play Scrabble. Make a photo collage.

Creativity . . . Just Between Friends

I felt joy when friends came into the hospital armed with love . . . and Seventeen magazines and Winchell doughnuts. It was neat when someone would buy birthday cards for me to use when special days came up. I'll never forget two girls who made it a weekly ritual to come and do my nails. What fun!

Friends like these equipped themselves not only with a Bible, but a box of Kleenex. They would sit, listen, pray. Since I could not use my hands, they would even wipe my eyes and blow my nose.

I remember one girl in particular on a painful night. Jackie knew I needed help. She simply climbed into bed, lay next to me, and held my hand. It felt good to have someone that near. In the quiet darkness she sang hymns. I'll never forget, "Man of Sorrows, what a Name. For the Son of God who came. Ruined sinners to reclaim. Hallelujah! What a Savior."

Those words sung quietly in the still night were a creative expression of comfort and care. Jackie empathized; she did not say, "I know what you're going through, Joni." She simply, quietly ministered.

And you know what? Jackie didn't disappear after the novelty of the hospital stay wore off—much like the four friends who stuck around to fix the roof after the crowd dispersed.

By the time three months in the hospital had passed, I noticed that only committed friends continued coming by. Visiting week in and week out called for not only commitment on their part, but creativity as well. Creativity, before and after the fact, is an exceptional quality in any friend.

What I've described involves helping a handicapped friend on a deeper level. There is an emotional involvement. You do more than merely reach out and touch in passing. Rather, you practice verse 4 in Philippians 2, "None of you should think only of his own affairs, but each should learn to see things from other people's point of view" (PHILLIPS, © 1958).

Philippians 2:3 says it more strongly, "Never act from motives of rivalry or personal vanity, but in humility, think more of each other than you do of yourselves" (PHILLIPS).

Putting muscle behind our words is following up our acts of kindness and gentleness with real humility. Humility means we are willing to identify with our handicapped friend. Just like the four friends who were willing to put their reputations on the line by tearing someone's roof apart, we will proudly identify with our disabled friend.

A Ministry of Refreshment

A few months ago I was in bed with a bad cold. Now being in bed when you're paralyzed is one thing, but with a cold it's something else—can you imagine the claustrophobia, the confinement? Besides, having a cold means my friends must rearrange their schedules to pour glasses of orange juice and help me blow my nose.

What friends! There is something wonderfully refreshing about the cool palm of a close friend on my fevered brow. They press their hands on my chest to help me cough. They wipe my tears when my eyes water. All in all, being around them is a real refreshment. My depressing cold doesn't make me feel as anxious or confined.

At this point I found myself thinking about the apostle Paul in his damp, cold prison. He must have succumbed at times to dark days of loneliness and disappointment. And in a letter to Timothy, the aging apostle describes his loneliness. He even asks Timothy to hurry and come before winter. He also must have ached with the chills since he asks in the letter for a heavy coat.

Paul's letter sounds so sad. It seems several of the friends he was counting on to testify on his behalf had deserted him. Paul was certainly not immune to the natural emotions that go along with confinement, sickness, or loneliness.

But the Apostle had a friend whom he knew would put a cool hand on his fevered brow. Paul mentions him, saying, "May the Lord show mercy to Onesiphorus because he has often refreshed me." Yes, the Lord gave Paul strength and renewal through one young man named Onesiphorus who humbly restored him.

God bless the people who take the time to refresh

another who is sick or lonely, anxious or confined. The very word "refresh" brings to mind an image of a hot, stale, stuffy room in which those inside are oppressed by the heat. Then someone walks in and opens a window, letting a cool breeze sweep the staleness away.

I thank the Lord for Onesiphorus. He helped give Paul a fresh perspective on his dreary surroundings. He wasn't well known. We don't hear from him again in Scripture. But he will be forever remembered for his ministry to the apostle Paul when he was at his weakest.

And I thank the Lord for my friends who let me borrow their hands. They aren't famous. Few others notice their efforts. But I will never forget them.

You can open the windows of someone's life today, bringing a fresh newness to the stale sameness of their difficult circumstances. Having a ministry of refreshment won our friend Onesiphorus a place in Scripture. In the same way you will win a place in God's heart and in the heart of a needy friend.

Don't Be Intimidated

Let me urge you to be aggressive as you throw open windows in the life of a disabled friend. Think back to the story of the paralyzed man who was lowered through a roof. Is there anything more creative than making a hole in a roof? Talk about overcoming inaccessibility! Like those four friends who were not willing to say, "This is impossible," don't be demoralized by a situation that *seems* to have no options. *There are alternatives*. Just put your thinking cap on. Don't be intimidated by an impossible situation.

And most importantly, don't be intimidated by an impossible attitude—even if it's your disabled friend's attitude.

I look back on my friends who were committed to success for me. When I got out of the hospital, one of my tough-loving friends was Diana. She had been around a lot when I was in the hospital and knew that I could draw. But she also knew I wasn't doing it.

I sat by the living room window, bored and depressed. At home, I didn't have an occupational therapist to push me. At first, Diana was intimidated by my lazy attitude, too fearful to push me, too afraid of my reactions. She helplessly watched as I lost myself in the past.

But one day that dramatically changed. I was sitting in the backyard looking at my old high school yearbook. I used to spend hours going over page after page of that book, calling up every memory, daydreaming about the way things used to be.

Well, that day Diana came by the farm. She caught me poring over my yearbook again. She paused a moment, hands on hips, then stomped up to me and declared, "Are you going to keep your nose stuck in that thing forever? You've got to start facing reality sometime!" With that, she grabbed my yearbook off my lapboard, slammed it shut, and walked away.

I don't remember what happened next. But I do remember being very angry. I felt she had no right to barge into my life and upset things so. She had no idea of what I had lost. What did she know about being paralyzed? What right did she have to tell me what to do?

I was seething. When my anger simmered down, I thought about her actions. Diana was my friend. She was envisioning success for me. And it would never be achieved if I spent my life reliving the past.

In fact, it was clear that Diana loved me enough to risk rejection. She refused to be held hostage by my wheelchair. She would not allow herself to be manipulated by my self-pity. Bitterness was not an attitude that intimidated her.

Because of her courage, she was able to do an impossible thing—confront me, a totally paralyzed person, with daring resolve. I am glad she was not afraid of confrontation.

Don't be alarmed if your disabled friend ignores—or worse—gets angry at your efforts to help. Disabled people are not paragons of virtue. For that matter, I don't know anyone, able-bodied or disabled, who is a paragon of virtue. People with disabilities are people—and most people I know struggle with resentment, bitterness, and even manipulation at times. Disabled people, like the able-bodied, are not above using others.

But here's an encouragement: If you hang in there, loving your embittered friend despite the abuses, no one will be able to accuse you of "doing your good deeds conspicuously to catch men's eyes" as it says in Matthew

6:1 (PHILLIPS). Love that hangs in there in the face of rejection can only be selfless love. No strings attached.

If you know someone with an impossible attitude, the creative and committed love you share can—and will—make a difference.

Nobody is an Impossible Case

It's people like Diana who help others, like me, envision life beyond the impossible. Stereotypes of who disabled people are and what they can do are being shattered everyday. A mentally-retarded young man, who is trained by an Olympic runner, now competes in marathons alongside able-bodied athletes. A deaf friend can live independently because her "hearing ear" dog alerts her to the sounds around her. A pretty, young quadriplegic now scuba dives 300 feet below the surface of the ocean. A college student, blind from birth, sews her own beautiful clothes. An architect paralyzed from the neck down is able to create new designs with the aid of a mechanical easel. A paraplegic leaves his wheelchair on a mountaintop and goes hang gliding.

Some would scoff at these examples as "super-crip" stories that few can identify with. But let's consider these examples: Cecile is 50 years old, attends college, and even propels her wheelchair around campus. Beth, who cannot dial a phone with her hands, has begun a telephone answering service. Jack, a quadriplegic, has recently married and plans to start a family. Bonnie, who has MS, heads a research department at a Christian ministry.

At one time, these people and their circumstances were considered "impossible cases." But their lives have become rich with possibility because caring and creative friends were there to help. They were friends who courageously searched for ways to help a disabled person achieve new goals and dreams.

You, too, can be one of those friends.

Don't Forget the Families

Allow me to interject an important thought. Frequently our concern and help for handicapped people begins and ends with the disabled individual. So please—do not neglect the family of the handicapped. Families may be in need of as much, if not more, help.

Let's consider just a few of the unique problems that the family of a handicapped youngster must face. Because of the day-to-day care for the child, fathers may have to take on a second job to pay for extra expenses. They struggle with the false guilt of fathering a handicapped child. They feel ashamed. And if the daily care is all consuming, fathers may feel neglected.

Mothers often struggle with guilt, too, because they feel they are neglecting home, husband, or other children. They are often left out of neighbourhood coffee mornings and are rarely included in parties and social events. People see them as too busy for such things. They find themselves refereeing fights between sisters. And mothers, sometimes overburdened, struggle with deep loneliness. They feel no one cares enough to offer a helping hand, or even to listen.

This is where you can step in. Take the initiative. Don't wait for an invitation. Rather, approach the family with an idea of how you would like to assist. Give them a creative plan of action like, "May I bring over a casserole on Tuesdays twice a month?" or "Why don't you let me come and stay with Steve for a couple hours every Thursday so that you have time to do some shopping or sign up for a class you've been wanting to attend. You can teach me his routines and he will be safe with me." Notice the sensitivity used in phrasing such questions—be careful not to offend the family's pride.

If the family doesn't need extra help (or if you are unable to get to their home), perhaps an offer to do ironing or bake cookies would be appreciated.

It bears repeating that a suggested plan of action makes it much easier for the family than a blanket statement, "Give me a call if I can help in any way." Even though sincere, that offer of help leaves the family in a rather awkward position. Would that friend rather help from their own house? When would be the best time? Would they rather cook or babysit? How about help with the cleaning or laundry? You can see why it may be an uncomfortable position for the mother of the handicapped child to approach this friend who has just given such a general offer of help.

It may be that you are part of a church that could

organize efforts to alleviate some of the strain on the family. What a difference this kind of caring can make as God's people share comfort through their work and His Word!

This is true in my own life. My family survived my painful disability because God brought along people to help. He led people across our path who assisted us in those day-to-day routines, who helped with the housework, and who took me on outings, giving my family a bit of a break.

You may know someone, some family, who needs that kind of help. If so, they are people who need not only comfort from God's Word but practical care from God's people. Let me encourage you to have some small part in making a difference in the life of that family.

Creativity. Commitment. Those are the keys.

Let me tell you about another friend who used creativity and commitment to help her disabled relative. Debbie, a girl I used to travel with, had a way of always finding time for others. It was never more clear than during a trip to central Florida where I spoke at a few churches and colleges. In spite of a busy schedule, I noticed that Debbie kept a very specific journal of not only everything I said, but everything we did and every place we went. She even made note of what we ate at which restaurant. Finally my curiosity got the best of me.

"What *are* you doing?" I asked, watching her hold a sandwich in one hand and notepad in the other.

"Oh," she said as she put her pencil behind her ear, "there's a special reason. You see, my grandmother is 90 years old, lives alone, and can't get out of her house. It's not easy finding creative things to do when I visit her. So I plan to tell her every little detail about this trip. That way she can experience the fun of this journey without even leaving her house."

"You're going to tell her about my hamburger?" I asked incredulously.

"Yeah," she said grabbing her pencil, "How 'bout telling me how it tastes?"

I shook my head and smiled. But I have to admit I was impressed. Debbie cared in such a time-consuming, thoughtful way. She was creative. She looked for options and alternatives. For her, a visit with her grandmother was not about to be impossibly boring. I took a look at her journal. I was certain it was going to take her a whole day to describe our short trip to Florida.

I learned something from Debbie. Even if our investment in the life of a disabled person is merely a weekly visit, you can be committed and creative.

Picture Debbie's visit to her grandmother. I can imagine her sitting on the edge of her grandmother's bed. I'm sure Debbie did more than pull up a chair and sit at the foot of the bed. She probably snuggled right up to her grandmother, slowly recounting every detail. Spending time. Sharing love. To her, a visit was a real investment—not only of her time, but of her love.

And friends who will use creativity are priceless. They are, in fact, close kin to the four friends who came up with an idea that no one else had thought of—"Hey, let's go through the roof!"

7
Charge It

Have you ever committed yourself to paying for something, and you weren't even sure how much it would cost? Repairs on a washing machine, a refrigerator, or even a trip to the doctor? You don't mind saying "Charge it." These are things that simply *must* be taken care of.

And there are needs of people that simply must be seen to. Even if it means committing ourselves without fully knowing the final cost. It's a rare person, indeed, who will make an open-ended commitment to someone in serious need, but such people, thankfully, do exist. Take, for example, the story of the Good Samaritan . . .

An expert in the law asked Jesus, "Who is my neighbor?"

In reply Jesus said: "A man was going down from Jerusalem to Jericho, when he fell into the hands of robbers. They stripped him of his clothes, beat him and went away, leaving him half dead. A priest happened to be going down the same road, and when he saw the man, he passed by on the other side. So too, a Levite, when he came to the place and saw him, passed by on the other side. But a Samaritan, as he traveled, came where the man was; and when he saw him, he took pity on him. He went to him and bandaged his wounds, pouring on oil and wine. Then he put the man on his own donkey, took him to an inn and took care of him. The next day he took out two silver coins, and gave them to the innkeeper. 'Look after him,' he said, 'and when I return, I will reimburse you for any extra expense you may have.' "

"Which of these three do you think was a neighbor to the man who fell into the hands of robbers?"

The expert in the law replied, "The one who had mercy on him."

Jesus told him, "Go and do likewise."

And those words are for us today: "Go and do likewise." The Good Samaritan saw the need, his emotions were moved, and he rolled up his sleeves to do all he could.

Quite different than the priest who barely noticed the man on the side of the road. He didn't have time. Others were expecting him. There were many committees looking to him for leadership, numerous meetings where people were counting on his input for their plans and programs.

Oh, to be sure, he felt bad for the suffering man as he passed by. What a shame that robbers would do such a thing! He wished he could stop, but he couldn't be late for his dinner appointment since his proposal was the first item on the agenda. Anyway, the man looked as though he were about to die. Why, the poor soul probably wouldn't survive being transported elsewhere for medical attention! So there really was nothing *he* could do.

Likewise, the reasoning of the Levite.

Then one of those Samaritans from the other side of the tracks came along. He cleaned and applied a balm to the wounds of the bleeding, beaten stranger. Without thinking, he ripped a strip of cloth from his own cloak—bandages were needed, and the stranger was naked without clothes of his own. It took a little longer since, after all, he wasn't a medical professional. He wiped the dirt and blood from his hands, not thinking about his own dry-cleaning bill.

Good thing he had the donkey with him. The injured stranger would have an uncomfortable ride, but the Samaritan didn't have any friends to help him carry a makeshift cot. Looking at those tender, open sores only made him wish he could shorten the trip to the inn.

The Good Samaritan did not simply leave the wounded man at the inn. Crossing off an appointment in his book, he stayed throughout the night, forfeiting his own sleep to give the man sips of water and touch a cool cloth to his wounds.

Here's the real clincher. The next morning not only did this generous man pay the bill at the inn, but he made a promise. He said he would be back to pay for any extra expenses. It wasn't enough that he had probably saved the man's life. He committed himself without knowing the final cost.

No wonder we were taught that story so often—we have a lot to learn from it! Not only about open-ended commitments, but also about compassion.

What Is Compassion?

Compassion. It's a word we usually link with deep feelings. We feel compassion when viewing a television special about refugees in Cambodia or starving families in Ethiopia. A little girl appears on the evening news pleading for a new liver to keep her alive, and we are filled with what we believe is compassion. An old man stands on the corner downtown, holding up a sign asking for work. He smiles and waves as you drive by. You feel compassion but cannot take time to stop.

A young mother struggles with the day-in, day-out care of her profoundly retarded three-year-old daughter. Her older children seem jealous of the attention their sister gets. Her husband seems distant. She has confided in you about her many difficulties. Your heart goes out to her, but how can you make a difference?

Compassion means much more than having "deep feelings." The word actually means, "with suffering." When you say you have compassion for someone, you are committing yourself to stand with that person. To have compassion is to agonize with him, suffering to the point of putting yourself in his shoes. It's easy to have strong feelings about someone's dilemma. But those feelings require a response, an action.

Just as Christ placed Himself on the cross in your stead, you, when you demonstrate compassion toward another, literally take upon yourself the cross that another is bearing.

Aren't you glad Jesus didn't stop at just feeling bad about your sin? We rejoice that the Lord went much further than merely feeling deeply sorry about our condition. He gave new meaning to the word *compassion*.

I know first-hand the value of having compassionate friends. When I first learned about my paralysis, I was glad for those friends who shared my burden. And I continued to need them when I later learned that my paralysis was permanent—that I would never walk again, that my hands would never work. Through each period of fresh grief, there were friends to share and bear my burden.

They cried with me. As the Good Samaritan must have done as he cleaned the wounds of the traveler, they would hold me in their arms and reassure me.

It was times like those that H. L. Mencken must have had in mind when he wrote, "There's always an easy solution to every human problem—neat, plausible, and wrong." My compassionate friends were quick to listen and slow to give solutions to my predicament. They knew I did not need advice.

Frankly, a lot of good advice was wasted on me back then. Good as it was, the counsel people gave me went right over my head. I was too emotionally turned upside down to make heads or tails out of their well-meaning words. It probably discouraged those dear friends. I am sure the advice made great sense to them. And, no doubt, they were anxious to see results—a smile on my face, or a happier attitude about my disability. But their compassion and commitment was not contingent on results.

When Your Friend Feels Like Crying

Compassion and open-ended commitment begins with allowing others time to cry. There is a time to weep and mourn, as the Bible says. We cannot expect newly disabled people to dry their tears and listen to our well-rehearsed Bible passages about suffering, hoping they will change overnight. They need time. Friends who lack real compassion find it difficult to give others time to adjust or accept a disability. Impatiently, they look for immediate results of their prayers and efforts.

But who can be impatient with the tears of someone who has lost so much? Especially one with a disability? For example, when I cry, I can't wipe my eyes. I lean forward and let the tears drop onto my lap. But that makes my nose run. And I can't even reach for a Kleenex. You can imagine, I'm a real mess when I cry. The frustration of it all makes me want to cry all the more!

So if there are rules on how to be a compassionate friend to a disabled person, the first would be to sincerely carry their emotional baggage. Allow your friend the freedom to express himself. Let him cry. Better yet, cry *with* him. We're even told to do that in Romans 12:15, ". . . weep with those who weep" (RSV).

When Your Friend Is Angry

But your friend may not be the crying type. Perhaps his emotions are better vented through anger. It's natural for a newly disabled person to shake his fist at God. "You say God's allowed this? Humph. With friends like Him, who needs enemies!" he may say.

Our reaction is to gasp in horror when we hear that kind of anger directed at God. But nothing your friend says is a surprise to God. He knows your friend's thoughts before they come out of his mouth. Review Psalm 139 as a reminder of how personally God knows each one of us. Phrases like ". . . you have searched me and you know me . . . you perceive my thoughts from afar . . . you are familiar with all my ways . . . before a word is on my tongue you know it completely, O Lord."

Allow your friend freedom to express his anger. It may even be directed at you some of the time. Commit yourself to hear it—and forget it. God doesn't need a defense lawyer. This is not the time to set any records straight. Nor is it the time to make a mental note of all that is said out of distress so that it can be brought up later. Remember that wonderful chapter of love in action, 1 Corinthians 13? One of the attributes of love is that we don't keep a record of wrongs—not for ourselves or anyone else. Not even for God! The same idea is voiced in Proverbs 10:12, ". . . love covers over all wrongs."

However, I must add an important and personal note. There was a certain point when several compassionate friends simply put their foot down and refused to put up with my anger or tears any further. They realized that was the loving thing to do. I'm sure they had to be extra sensitive to the Spirit's leading and to my condition to do such a thing. But I'm glad their commitment was deep enough to risk my rejection.

When Your Friend Is Having Doubts

Also, give the disabled person room for doubt. We all doubt at one time or another, and I wonder why we refuse to admit it (as though it were shameful). There certainly are examples of Christians who doubted in the Bible. The disciple Thomas said in so many words, "I don't believe it, but I sure would like to." The father of the boy with an evil spirit said, "I do believe; help me overcome my unbelief." Somehow I think Jesus read his heart and understood his quandary.

Can you understand how easy it would be to doubt God if you just learned you had a terminal illness? Can you empathize with someone who only recently discovered he had to have his leg amputated? Doubts are common among the disabled. Don't be caught off-guard. Have faith on the behalf of your friend who lacks it. God can even give him faith to still doubt—and yet believe.

Look again at the story in Luke 10. It is significant that the Samaritan didn't show his love by taking the injured man straight to church. Instead he took him to an inn where real healing could begin. There were no platitudes, no dropping a coin in the coffer. No, the Good Samaritan not once trivialized the injured man's misfortune with prepackaged Bible verses or a pat on the head.

The injured man may have cried. He may have been angry. He could have even doubted God. The Good Samaritan, however, showed the compassionate, committed response. But what he did along the road was only the beginning.

What about Dedication?

And this is what makes the Good Samaritan story so extraordinary—what happens after the initial encounter. Having nursed the injured man through the night, the Samaritan leaves, saying, "Charge it." He commits himself to the care of this man, without even knowing what that commitment entails!

That might be the depth of dedication required of many of us as we reach out to help our handicapped friend. We must be able to say, "I'm here and I want to help. Whatever it means, I'm here for you."

Such was the case in Acts 3. A handicapped man sat for 40 years by the Beautiful Gate of the temple, begging for money. At best, he could simply hope that those alms would sustain him in his meager existence.

But Peter and John came on the scene. They refused to meet this man's need superficially. Instead of just dropping a coin into his outstretched hand, they went a step further and gave this man the ability to earn his living.

We can bring about miracles of a different sort in the life of our handicapped friend. We can offer much more than band-aid solutions to his problems. As Christians we are called to enact radical solutions. We are to do more than heal the hurt slightly. And the time and energy involvement may be great.

The Lord will make it very clear if you are to become this involved in the life of your handicapped friend. I could almost guarantee you from personal experience that this is something that will evolve quite naturally as your friendship deepens. It's not as though one day you'll wake up with a degree in sociology. Rather, taking one step at a time, you begin to envision success for your friend . . . and commit yourself to help him achieve it.

How does it happen? There was a young couple in church whose first child was multiply handicapped. Because of the nature of the handicaps, Nathan could only survive in the intensive care unit of a children's hospital over 40 miles from his parents' home. This meant that his parents, Dennis and Kathleen, would make daily trips to be near their son and aid in his care.

About the time of Nathan's first birthday, the insurance limit had been reached. Nathan had to be institutionalized as a ward of the state or his parents would have to assume his complete care.

There was no question as to their decision—they would, of course, assume the care for their child. It was at this point that the church took a more active role. Until this time, close friends had lent a hand now and then. A few had visited the hospital with Kathleen and assisted with Nathan's daily care. Others had occasionally helped out by preparing meals.

But now things were different. Friends set themselves to the task of learning, along with Kathleen, the many nursing routines that were now necessary. Learning how to properly exercise, medicate, feed, and suction Nathan was only the beginning. They took on full-time responsibility of this precious baby boy.

In order for Nathan to be able to come home, the living room—the only room large enough for the medical equipment—had to be turned into an intensive care unit. From that room, life went on for Dennis and Kathleen and their baby Nathan.

The commitment increased. One woman made it her ministry to coordinate the numerous tasks. Meals were taken in every night. Women from the church came in every day to clean, sterilize water, work on the medical equipment, do laundry—whatever they could to help. It was particularly humbling to Kathleen when one day each week a Christian friend drove up in her Rolls Royce to clean toilets, bathtubs, and floors.

Because Nathan had to be suctioned every twenty minutes, another friend spent two nights each week with him, giving Kathleen a chance for a solid night's sleep. These specially-trained friends made it possible for Kathleen to leave the house once in awhile, even just for shopping or an occasional lunch.

You're probably saying, "But that's a big church. They've got all sorts of people to help out." No, the church was made up of 150 people. And these people were committed, even though they had no idea of the eventual results of their labors. You see, God didn't choose to do physical healing in Nathan's life on this earth. He finally went to be with Jesus.

But pulling together, these many people were saying, "Charge it. No matter what it costs. We're committed to this family and will help in any way we can." And they did. What a tremendous ministry and practical demonstration of unconditional love and unlimited friendship!

What will it cost you to have an open-ended commitment to your friend? No one knows. Not even your disabled friend. But the Lord Jesus knows . . . and remembers. Just ask the Good Samaritan.

8
After All These...
Put on Love

"Therefore, as God's chosen people, holy and dearly loved, clothe yourselves with compassion, kindness, humility, gentleness and patience."

As I sat with my friends at a Bible camp high in the Rockies, Colossians 3:12 began to take on new meaning. I mentally checked off each word as the speaker read.

Compassion . . . kindness . . . humility . . . gentleness . . . patience. Now, looking at this list rather casually, one might think the traits mean pretty much the same thing. But the Holy Spirit does not waste words. Each has special significance. So far, we have seen these words find specific meaning in each of our stories.

What *compassion*—what deep feeling turned into action—Christ showed in his treatment of the woman with the issue of blood who touched Him. Even though she stopped Jesus on His way, He was gentle with her, taking care of her urgent need. Not only did she find the physical healing she so needed, but the Savior took time to stop, to talk with her, and to assure her that her sins were forgiven. In the same way, we learned how we can show compassion to disabled people who are mere acquaintances, meeting the simplest of their needs in passing.

Then we couldn't help but admire those four friends who put their reputations on the line, helped their disabled friend, and found a creative solution for crowd control! Ripping up a roof and then fixing it was an unusual act of kindness, to say the least. And kindness often takes shape through creativity and commitment. We learned that a friendship with a disabled person deepens as your creative acts of kindness help him deal better with his handicap.

Oh, and the *humility* and *gentleness* of that committed man—the Good Samaritan. He put to death any pride and selfishness, going the extra mile no matter what the cost. The Samaritan not only met the initial need; he didn't rest until the job was completed! He even anticipated the special needs that might arise after he had left the inn. We learned from him how to be a friend with open-ended commitment.

Cultivating Patience

And now we move to the last of these Christlike characteristics—*patience*. We are not going to get very far in
our Christian walk if we are moved with compassion to
do a deed of kindness—in humility and gentleness—but
we do it impatiently, in a huff.

I can understand how that happens. I've known people
who started to help me, only to have things fall apart.
They begin with the best of intentions, and things go well
for a while. And then suddenly they don't! The kindness
and gentleness, humility and compassion get tangled up
with frustrations and failures. Everything becomes a big
inconvenience. And what few Christlike qualities were
demonstrated become lost in impatience.

Talk about feeling like an imposition! Instead of being
on the same team, we were at opposite ends. I became
less of a person and more of a "project." I found myself
making apologies about the littlest things—things I
couldn't control and certainly didn't have any reason to
apologize for.

How important patience is. Not only are we to put on
compassion, humility, kindness, and gentleness, but also
patience. That's the icing on the cake! Patience perseveres.

I had a chance to witness this kind of patience at the
same Bible camp in the Rockies. Vicky Olivas, also a
quadriplegic in a wheelchair, shared a cabin with me. She
has many, if not more, needs than I do, and our friend
Rana was helping her with her everyday routines.

It was my first opportunity to get a close-up look at

the way someone else takes care of a quadriplegic. I watched Rana empty Vicky's leg bag, adjust her position in the chair, give her glasses of water, put on her jacket, take off her jacket, push her here and there, feed her, exercise her . . . the list could go on!

Rana kept doing kindnesses, in humility, with much gentleness. And she continued doing it all week long, showing patience. The result? Well, Vicky was greatly helped. But there was more. We saw real growth in Rana as she clothed herself with this quality of Jesus. And we benefitted by watching.

A Closer Look at King David

Vicky and Rana reminded me of a story in 2 Samuel chapters 1–9. King David was at the height of his power and influence. After years of serving King Saul faithfully, David had now come to the throne. Forced to run for his life during King Saul's reign, he refused to retaliate. And when he learned of King Saul's death, the Bible tells us that he, along with all of his men, tore his clothes, mourned, and fasted.

David was also weeping for Jonathan, Saul's son. He had been David's best friend for years. Jonathan had been next in line for the crown, but now he was gone, and David grieved.

David did many new things as king. He brought the ark—the symbol of God's presence—back to the city. He did what was just and right for all his people. And Jerusalem saw blessings on every side.

It was at this point David asked the question, "Is there anyone still left of the house of Saul to whom I can show kindness for Jonathan's sake?" (9:1). Even though he had every kingly right to destroy any of Jonathan's heirs, he wanted to show mercy and generosity.

Ziba, an elderly servant of Saul's, shuffled into the king's chambers. Shy about revealing too much, he timidly gave the answer. Yes, there was someone left. Jonathan's son, Mephibosheth.

Then in the same breath Ziba added, "He is crippled in both feet."

What went through David's mind? Did he know what the book of Leviticus had to say about handicapped people—the stigma, the isolation, the lack of acceptance and privileges? If he knew it, it didn't make any difference—pure joy and excitement showed on his face. Mephibosheth, his best friend's son, was alive!

But Mephibosheth was shocked. King David wanted to show him kindness? How could that be? He deserved banishment. Not only that, he was severely disabled. Yet he was invited not only to eat at the king's table, but to *live* within the palace. Incredible!

"Why me?" Mephibosheth replied. "I'm a nobody." But the king had spoken. It was as good as done.

King David and Mephibosheth developed an intimate friendship as David provided practically—and we can assume, spiritually—for this man who was crippled in both feet. David, in the best way, partnered patience with those other Christlike qualities we've talked about—kindness, humility, compassion, and gentleness. And both he and Mephibosheth benefitted.

Making It Practical

There are still "King Davids" today. God gives many the ability—and the desire—to provide lifelong care for someone with a disability. It may be the parents of a beautiful newborn with cerebral palsy. They know of the complications which will crowd their family life. There will be extra medical costs and responsibilities. Other members of the family may feel neglected. The pressures of social isolation and financial strain will be tremendous.

But God has given them this special child. And together they are committed to her love and care. Day in and day out, as God gives the grace, they clothe themselves in patience to do again what they did yesterday . . . and the day before . . . and in the many days to come.

That's the kind of patience that I saw in Rana during that Bible camp. I noticed that serving Vicky was almost second nature to Rana. There was no fanfare, no glory-seeking. She just did what needed to be done. And as with any of us who are severely disabled, things had to be done repeatedly for Vicky. But Rana was not keeping count.

Patience and perseverance are needed at this level. Don't expect life to always "come up roses." If your disabled friend is going to live with you, or if you intend to provide ongoing care and support, there are bound to be misunderstandings. To protect your friendship (or your family relationship), you will need:

- to take occasional breaks from one another
- to talk openly and honestly about your relationship, your expectations of each other (especially if either of you feels used or manipulated)
- to pray together, asking for God's grace
- to clearly outline each other's responsibilities for organizing respite attendant care, ordering medical supplies, shopping, cooking, making appointments, arranging transportation, etc.
- in short, to mutually agree to look out for one another's interests

The temptation will be to give up in the face of frustration. Take heart. You're not the only one. Hebrews 4:15–16 says, "For we do not have a high priest who is unable to sympathize with our weaknesses, but we have one who has been tempted in every way, just as we are—yet was without sin. Let us then approach the throne of grace with confidence, so that we may receive mercy and find grace to help us in our time of need."

Jesus was tempted in *every* way like we are. He was tempted to slack off a little because He was so tired. He was tempted to snap back at His disciples when they didn't seem to listen to what He was saying. He may have felt like saying, "Oh, what's the use? No one appreciates me anyway." Feeling sorry for Himself must have been a big temptation. He was acquainted with each and every negative emotion we experience. He knew them all and yet yielded to none.

When we feel we're at the end of our rope, we can go to Him for help. He'll be there with His mercy and grace.

A New Attitude about Serving

Somebody once asked a friend of mine who assists me with a lot of my personal care, "What does it feel like to have given three years of your life to serving Joni?"

I wasn't around when the question was asked, but my friend told me that she cringed—the tone of the question sounded so somber and pitiful. But that question is asked of many. Perhaps of someone who takes care of an elderly mother or a sick child. Sometimes people will say that a wife has given her disabled husband the best years of her life, or a man has given himself in "tireless service" to a friend with multiple sclerosis.

But what does "tireless service" really mean? May a friend who assists me do the replying?

"What does it feel like, you say, to give three years of my life in order to serve Joni?"

The person nodded, as if expecting a reply from a noble, suffering saint.

"Well," she took a deep breath, "I can't say I've given three years of my life to serve Joni."

The questioner seemed perplexed.

"My service hasn't been only to Joni." My friend continued, "It's more for the Lord. Colossians 3:23 says, 'Whatever your task, work heartily, as serving the Lord and not men, knowing that from the Lord you will receive the inheritance as your reward; you are serving the Lord Christ' " (RSV).

"But . . . but, don't you get tired?"

My friend smiled, nodding. "Sure, it's tiring. Even exhausting. For me *and* for Joni." Then she added thoughtfully, "But it doesn't have to be tiresome."

My friend couldn't have said it better. She hasn't "given up" her life to help me. She's responding to the circumstances God has placed her in. And I could say the same thing for my husband, Ken. He hasn't committed his life to emptying my leg bag or cutting up the food on my plate, lifting me in and out of my wheelchair, or turning me on my side at night. He has committed himself to the Lord. And to me—the *real me* apart from my disability.

These people are serving the Lord by helping me. And how can service to Christ be a tiring, boring effort? To men maybe, to organizations often . . . even to causes. But to Christ? How could that be? He who has given us all things for life, enrichment, and enjoyment? Jesus, who has suffered so much to secure for us our salvation, should be a joy to serve!

An Important Personal Note

But I have to admit that the joy is sometimes hard to find. For instance, Ken and I, when tackling problems which relate to my disability, often struggle with how closely those "handicap problems" are attached to "me." Let me explain . . .

Sometimes it helps to think of my disability as not "mine" at all. Ken and I have learned to team up against problems which exist outside of us as a couple. By determining to distance ourselves from the situation, we regroup in order to deal with it head-on.

Emotionally, we step back from the wheelchair which gets a flat tire, the batteries which run dry while at a shopping mall, the leg bag which springs an embarrassing leak. It is Ken and I teaming up and tackling it—the disability. We can better cope with it that way.

But coping isn't always easy. Sometimes problems which relate to my disability are an intimate part of *who I am*. Although there are times when we are able to surgically disassociate ourselves from the mechanical breakdowns, we can't always separate ourselves from other aspects of my handicap. For example, sometimes I struggle with not being able to rub my husband's back, help myself to a glass of lemonade, or hike with Ken in the mountains. It also bothers Ken that I can't do these things. These are the times when we can only sigh and say, "Well, when we got married, we agreed, 'Love me, love my disability.' "

The rule of thumb? Simply put, there is no rule. Each

inconvenience, each struggle is very individual, made more so by the emotions of the individual moment. When frustrations mount, whether they are an intimate part of me or simply circumstances we find ourselves in, Ken and I pray for grace and guidance. It's the Lord who sees us through.

I hope this encourages you to look on the bright side of helping someone with a disability. Remember, your work will be tiring, but it doesn't have to be tiresome. You will become weary, but your service does not have to be wearisome. "The joy of the Lord is your strength," it says in Nehemiah 8:10 and that joy is yours to experience each morning as you wake up wondering where you will find the strength to do your tasks.

An intimate relationship with a disabled friend or family member can be a special way to discover what real love is all about. As you both do your work heartily as to the Lord, every day can have purpose, challenge, and meaning.

A Final Word from Joni

May I share one last word? Beside compassion, kindness, humility, and gentleness, Colossians 3:14 adds one more significant word: "And over all these virtues put on *love*, which binds them all together in perfect unity."

Jim Wright, a teacher of the Book of Colossians, compares these qualities to a hand. Those first five virtues could be the five fingers. Love would be the skin, covering those virtues and holding them all together.

To do our work begrudgingly is to do no service at all. As 1 Corinthians 13 puts it, "If I . . . have not love, I gain nothing."

Before you put this book down to apply the insights

you've gained, pray about your motives. And read the passage in 1 Corinthians 13 about unconditional love: "This love of which I speak is slow to lose patience—it looks for a way of being constructive. It's not possessive: it is neither anxious to impress nor does it cherish inflated ideas of its own importance. Love has good manners and does not pursue selfish advantage. It is not touchy. It does not keep account of evil or gloat over the wickedness of other people. On the contrary, it shares the joy of those who live by the truth. Love knows no limit to its endurance, no end to its trust, no failing of its hope; it can outlast anything. Love never fails" (PHILLIPS).

Put on love. That is friendship unlimited!

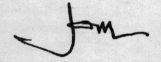